WEST COUNTRY LAN~~~~~~~~~~.
THE MENDIPS

Cover: Waldegrave Pool
Overleaf: Mendip Edge, View from Draycott Sleights across the Levels

WEST COUNTRY LANDSCAPES

The Mendips

Robin & Romey Williams

EX LIBRIS PRESS

First published in 1996 by
EX LIBRIS PRESS
1 The Shambles
Bradford on Avon
Wiltshire

Typeset in 10 point Palatino
Design and typesetting by Ex Libris Press

Cover printed by Shires Press, Trowbridge
Printed in Britain by
Cromwell Press, Broughton Gifford, Wiltshire

ISBN 0 948578 74 2

For Bryony, Sebastian and Megan.
May they appreciate the freedom and beauty of Mendip as they grow up.

Acknowledgements
We would like to thank our interviewees and all who helped with information,
including Janet Boyd, John Boyd, Brian Prewer, David Sheldon and Bill Small
who, with great patience, answered our questions and provided us with a wealth
of information and anecdotes about this fascinating area and its people.
Thankyou also to English Nature and the Somerset Wildlife Trust staff who
provided basic facts about changes and the background to various important
policies which have taken effect over the years; and to many others, too numerous to mention, who have contributed thoughts and knowledge to the book.

CONTENTS

Series Introduction

The present series, West Country Landscapes, deals with significant and identifiable landscapes of the south-western counties. These contain two National Parks – Exmoor and Dartmoor – and several Areas of Outstanding Natural Beauty.

Our preference is for areas of the West Country which are perhaps less well documented than the National Parks, and for books which offer a complete picture of a particular landscape. We favour, too, an author who is sufficiently well acquainted with his or her chosen landscape to present his story in the round and with an ease in the telling which belies his depth of knowledge. Authors for West Country Landscapes have been chosen with this in mind.

The plan of each book is quite simple: the subject's underlying geology is the starting point. From this basis we are led to an understanding of that landscape's topography, of its flora and fauna and of the particular pattern of human settlement to which it gives rise – natural history followed by human history, in other words. Then we may look more closely at people and traditions, and at the interaction between individuals and the landscape – perhaps as expressed in literature and folklore. Throughout each account, there is constant reference to what may be seen on the ground today.

West Country landscapes vary greatly – this is part of their great appeal. Likewise authors vary in their enthusiasms and areas of expertise. All these factors have a bearing on the books which we publish in the West Country Landscapes series. The books are substantial but succinct, well rounded but readable accounts of noteworthy pockets of the West Country, each with its particular characteristics and each penned by individually minded authors.

Any comments and suggestions from readers will be welcomed by the publishers.

Roger Jones, Editor

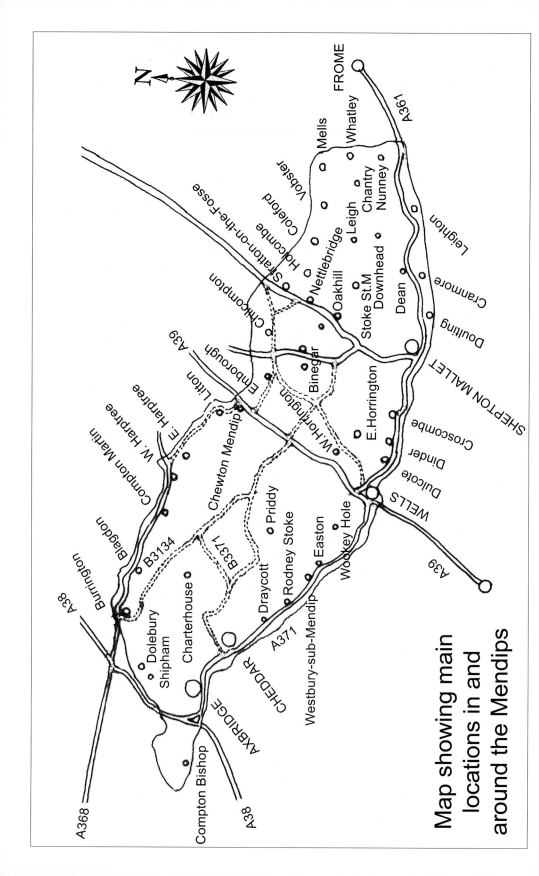

Map showing main locations in and around the Mendips

1 An Ancient Landscape

Introduction

Stretching thirty miles across the old county of Somerset, from the Valley of the River Frome in the east to near the Bristol Channel in the west, the Mendip Hills is one of those distinctive areas which every so often characterise our varied and beautiful countryside. The gleaming pale limestone gives it its character, with a sometimes featureless plateau on top, but with dramatically slashed and folded edges enough to please anyone, sharply separating the flat lands of the moors and levels eight-hundred feet below from the rolling lands of the north.

The landscape of Mendip is amongst the oldest inhabited parts in the country, mined for its rich minerals since earliest times and providing shelter, woods and hunting above the surrounding marshes and wastes of what is now known as the Somerset Levels. Often militarily strategic, valued for its stone and minerals, extraordinarily beautiful in its special way, eighty-four square miles of Mendip was designated an Area of Outstanding Natural Beauty (AONB) in 1972.

In 1974 the Mendip Hills were split between Somerset and the new County of Avon, although it now appears likely that this area will return to the ancient boundaries of Somerset in due course.

But it is far more than a man-made boundary simply setting some of the country apart. Physically it is quite different from the surrounding countryside, being visible as a long ridge from all directions. Indeed it has rightly been described as a wall between the Levels and north Somerset.

Mendip has its own climate, wet and often shrouded in mist, as we knew to our cost when we lived up above Wells, near Binegar. One of us would set off for work in Bristol, leaving the house wreathed in cloud, descend to a beautiful sunny day and return to enter fog again. The other would have spent the day in that depressing, particularly clingy type of mist in which the area specialises. It is cold and late on top; our garden was a month behind Wells a few hundred feet below. Yet when the sun did come out it was spectacularly beautiful, with a wonderful display of wild flowers. Mendip's largely limestone bedrock creates its own special fauna and flora.

In some parts there is a high rainfall, contrasting with the meagre nature of that falling on the Levels. Indeed, Priddy is said by those who live there to have the highest rainfall in the West.

But for all these apparent drawbacks it is a magic place, unexpected in its rugged summit, great outcrops of limestone and spectacular gorges, in a county of predominantly rolling, manicured hills or great sea-level plains. Coming up through the bedlam of Cheddar to the peace and fresh air of the top is like finding a piece of the Derbyshire Peaks set in the middle of Hertfordshire. The impact is amazing and the feeling of marvel increases with acquaintance. It is not a place where familiarity breeds contempt. True lovers of Mendip are noted for the passion with which they seek new places and views, as well as constantly revisiting the old and familiar.

What and where is Mendip?

The Mendip Hills is a massif of limestone and sandstone which runs east and west across the middle of the old County of Somerset, on the northern fringe of the Somerset Levels, reaching over one-thousand feet in height in a part where the adjacent land is at sea-level. It is one of those areas of the countryside which is so obviously different from its surrounds as to be a recognisable entity and an attraction in its own right. The Royal Forest of Mendip belonged to the Crown for many centuries and the area is now one of the major tourist attractions of the West Country. It has probably been used by, and connected with, man for longer than any other part of Somerset, in spite of its apparently unspoiled nature and innate wildness.

An examination of Government and other official leaflets, old books and discussions with local societies can raise varying opinions as to the actual extent of Mendip as such. The map on page 8 shows our vision of the area. The present AONB covers the western half of the great raised massif which forms the core of what many people consider to be Mendip. The AONB spills over north of the raised part onto Blagdon and Chew Valley Lakes far below. We cannot see that this is either historically, geographically or naturally a part of heartland Mendip.

Controversy also arises at each end, both west and east. To the west there is no doubt that Steep Holm in the Bristol Channel, and Brent Knoll on the M5, are extensions of the same rock formations from which Mendip is made, but there has to be some form of 'ring-fence' for any place and both these are geographically separate. Brent Knoll and Brean Down are surrounded by sea or the Levels. The main mass of stone, which is the visual sign of Mendip, starts at Crook Peak in the west and ends before reaching Frome in the east, although Frome may like to think of itself as a Mendip township. Anyone who knows the area is aware of the change in the countryside which occurs to the west here, from a great plateau to smaller rolling hills.

Wells has been included because physically it stands on the edge of Mendip and part of its wealth came from mining the hills above.

The rest of the area is as seen on a map, where the contours rise sharply from the surrounding lower levels. It is this which gives such panoramic views from so many points.

So the edges of 'our' Mendip range from Rowberrow in the west by way of Burrington, East Harptree, and Chilcompton on the top, through to Nunney in the east. Along the south the boundary goes by way of Cranmore to Shepton Mallet, Wells, and through the strawberry villages to Cheddar and Compton Bishop. From the south Mendip looks like some great whale, extending on the horizon from Crook Peak in the west to well beyond Wells' television mast to the east, a magnificent sweep of wild country.

Geology

The area is particularly interesting geologically, with two distinct rock types appearing on the surface and having differing effects on the location of water, in a region of considerable rainfall. The Old Red Sandstone is impermeable and is the only part where water is found running on the surface. The bulk of Mendip is Carboniferous Limestone, seamed with deep gorges such as Cheddar and Burrington Combe. Limestone dissolves in waters containing carbon dioxide so most streams run in beds well below the surface, with little or no trace up above. A particular feature of this countryside is the presence of swallet holes down which the surface waters plunge to the streams underneath. These waters emerge in springs or rivers at the foot of the escarpment, in places such as Wookey and Cheddar.

Geologically Mendip is formed of Palaeozoic rocks, in a long ridge which runs from near Frome in the east out to the islands of Steep Holm and Flat Holm in the Bristol Channel. This ridge reaches over one-thousand feet in three places, particularly impressive when it is seen ascending straight up from sea-level on the Somerset peat moors.

Old Red Sandstone occurs on the surface in four areas of Mendip, most spectacularly on Black Down, where a walk up the hill from the riding stables with the transition from limestone to sandstone results in a quite noticeable change of colour and type of vegetation, as well as insect life. The colour change is seen most clearly on the surface of a bare track which runs uphill from Tynings Farm to Mendip Lodge Wood, edging the woods at Rowberrow Warren. The other areas are Beacon Hill, above Westbury-sub-Mendip, North Hill, by Priddy Nine Barrows, and Pen Hill, where the TV mast stands above Wells. The rest is hard, white limestone, everywhere coloured spectacularly with lichens.

The eastern area of Mendip is largely conventional grassland, with little or no surface rock, and hedges rather than walls. The western area, particularly in that great spectacular spread from Cheddar to Burrington, has much exposed rock, clouds of wild-flowers and an interesting and varied insect population, as well as many good examples of stone walling. The two areas differ greatly.

Land Use

History and Prehistory
Mendip abounds with signs of those who used the land and lived here in the distant past. Stone Age hunters, people from the Iron and Bronze Ages, Saxons and Romans, have all left their mark. Tumuli, long barrows, mysterious circles and early signs of mining are everywhere, particularly in the western parts. Mendip was a Royal hunting forest under many kings. Man has used Mendip well, though perhaps it has not always served him so kindly.

Farming
The area has long been famous for its sheep, on which much of the wealth of the area depended in former times. The business continues to this day and it is not unusual to come round a corner and find a great flock flowing like water ahead of a couple of dogs.

But nowadays more of western Mendip is ploughed up and this is continuing with the growing pressure on farm incomes. Pigs may be seen rooting up fields above Draycott, living out on free range. These creatures have been found to be excellent precursors to grain crops, turning over the ground and fertilising it.

As elsewhere, there have been changes brought about by milk quotas, encouraging larger but fewer herds, as some farmers have gone out of business and others have bought their quotas. Many more beef cattle are seen and the eastern part of Mendip retains its typically permanent grass-land appearance, green and fresh from the high rainfall of the area.

A typical corner of West Mendip.

Horticulture

Perhaps the biggest changes have taken place in horticulture, most of which occurs on the southern edges, typically on the old strawberry slopes of the villages from Rodney Stoke to Axbridge.

Strawberries used to be the principal crop, with fields also devoted to early anemones. They are grown still, but not to the same intensity. In the old days the Strawberry Special took the crops up to Birmingham and London by the main line. Cheddar strawberries were noted for their quality, taste and earliness, but a period of rapid change followed. Beeching introduced his infamous cuts and the stations and line closed in the late 1960s. No longer was the life of the growers bound to the departure of the train.

Then came cheap and wide-ranging availability of air flights round the world. Strawberries were flown in from Israel and elsewhere, making them available for most of the year and cutting the market for the sale of Cheddar fruit outside the valley. Efforts were made to hang on, with polythene tunnels and sheeting, but to little avail. Even the quality started to suffer in the search for larger and more reliable yields. The old strawberry varieties, Royal Sovereign and others, were large and delicious but somewhat variable in yield and often marked, as well as being susceptible to disease. Nowadays, the supermarkets appear to prefer uniform, brightly coloured fruit and vegetables to tasty ones; the bland beauty to the delicious one which varies in shape.

Finally the growers realised they were beaten and concentrated on the local market, much swollen at just the right time of the year by the large tourist trade. More and more roadside stalls and increasingly sophisticated farm shops started to capitalise on this. Other crops were grown to complement these sales and the area has diversified considerably.

Mushrooms are grown commercially in large quantities, and a vineyard produces excellent quality white wine on the slopes above Axbridge.

The soil is perfect for growing market garden crops, with good rainfall and some of the highest sunshine levels in the country on the warm southern slopes. It should continue to support a growing and flourishing trade aimed directly at local and tourist markets.

Woodland
One of the features of Mendip is the amount of woodland, much of it deciduous, though, inevitably, conifers have been planted in considerable tracts as commercial crops. A proportion of these deciduous woods is managed by various conservation bodies, who are trying to develop a reasonable strategy for their survival as islands of shelter for insects, bird-life and flora. This is difficult to achieve because few individual blocks are large enough for really effective management in the conservation sense. These woodland tracts have been retained for a variety of reasons, as shelter around water-sources for the water companies, because they are too costly to convert to grassland, or because conservation bodies have bought them. Unfortunately, only the conifers are currently justifiable as true economic investments, a source of nervousness to those who love them and see their value as an essential part of our countryside.

Uses for wood have changed greatly since the war, with much reduced requirements for hurdles, stakes and rick fastenings. Labour costs are so high that it is difficult to justify coppicing or thinning deciduous woods except as part of a conservation programme, and even then it is difficult to find the money. Fresh efforts need to be made to look for new outlets if the existing woods are to survive and evolve. Firewood, garden and fence stakes, woven hazel fencing, charcoal manufacturing and others come to mind but a great deal more thought needs to be given to the problem of retaining these, our very lungs, as forests have been described.

Many people hate the dank, dark conifers, but others thoroughly enjoy the privilege of walking through them. Sadly, it is not possible to take anything for granted nowadays, so let us hope that future casualties do not include our magnificent deciduous Mendip woods, or further privatisation removing the right to walk through Forestry Commission plantations.

Remnants of older woodland on the edges of new plantations.

Beneath the Surface

Mendip has always been famed for its mineral wealth, with lead being mined by the Romans and before, and continuing until less than a hundred years ago. Equally, its stone has long been praised and heavily used, from the polished stone known as Draycott Marble and used for fine fittings and table tops, to the creamy Doulting Stone which raised Wells Cathedral and both Glastonbury and Bath Abbey to sublime heights.

But nowadays Mendip is perhaps best known for the controversy surrounding its limestone quarries, used for building many of the country's motorways and more and more rapidly eating into the heart of the hills. The quantities being extracted are rising inexorably, causing the expansion of the quarries and alterations to the horizon as rock is removed. There are serious worries that this is also having a detrimental effect on the watertable of the area, with consequences which will go far beyond the bounds of Mendip. But, for all that, stone quarries are major employers in the area, with many families depending on their continuing existence.

Lead has been a major factor in attracting people to Mendip since Roman times. The ore lies close to the surface and has been mined intensively over many centuries, the evidence of the diggings can be seen in 'gruffy' ground in many parts. The main concentration is in western Mendip, round Priddy and Charterhouse.

With the problems of digging more deeply, mining dwindled during the eighteenth century when costs exceeded sales. Lead mining revived during the middle of the nineteenth century, with the old tips being reworked by new technology to extract the large amounts left behind as spoil. There are remarkably few reminders of this vital industry, but the long flue tunnels at Charterhouse are worth exploring, and a chimney remains virtually intact at Smitham Hill near East Harptree.

Another mineral which enjoyed considerable success on Mendip is calamine, a zinc-bearing ore providing a raw material for brass. This was mined extensively round Shipham from the eighteenth century for sixty or seventy years before also becoming uneconomic.

The other gold which lies beneath the surface is liquid. The great mass of Mendip is limestone, soluble in carbon dioxide solution and allowing water to percolate through the surface to underground streams and lakes, providing large reserves of water. The same effect has carved vast and extended cave systems, often reached only by the swallet holes which carry water underground. These are a source of joy to an ever-growing number of pot-holers and cavers. Mendip is a famous centre for this sport, again with the concentration on western Mendip.

So the ground beneath is as important as the surface, economically speaking, providing a living for many people, leisure for others and giving a unique character to the area.

16

Mendip is long famous for the attractions of Cheddar with its Gorge, shops and caves; Wookey caves, paper-making and fairground collection; the beauties of Axbridge and the great cathedral and medieval buildings of Wells. Gliding, horse-riding and walking are some of the pastimes which depend on the Mendip countryside for their enjoyment.

For a 'wild and desolate' area it has a remarkable range of activities, ways of making a living and of spending leisure hours. For those of us who live near or on it, there is no other place which compares with Mendip. It has its own particular beauty, climate and style – an ancient land which has managed to retain its atmosphere and way of life in modern times. There is a sense of history everywhere, a feeling for the 'old' people buried in the barrows, the miners who dug so much of the surface and the Roman legions who marched across the cold plateau, of abbots and poachers, woodsmen and shepherds.

Market Cross at Shepton's heart.

2 A Snapshot of Mendip

Roads

Mendip is a truly rural area with comparatively few roads, not many towns and villages, and a generally sparsely inhabited appearance. Away from the built-up areas, houses are scattered, mostly great gaunt farmhouses, self-contained, with their own yards and cottages.

The main roads run around the perimeter below the escarpment, circling the massif. The A38, the old-time artery of the West Country taking people from Bristol to Taunton and Exeter, forms part of the western boundary, slicing through Mendip between Wavering Down and Shute Shelve Hill. The A368 follows the northern edge of Mendip from the A38 at Churchill to Compton Martin, before wandering north, away from the hills. In the south the A361 leaves the A38 at Cross, meandering through the strawberry lands of Cheddar, Draycott, Rodney Stoke and Westbury to Wells, then continues through quarrying country beyond Shepton Mallet to Frome.

The centre of Mendip is bisected, north to south, by the A39 from Wells to Chewton Mendip. The AONB is to the west of this road and there is a quite different feel to the country on either side. The west is what people have come to think of as typical Mendip, with stone walls, outcrops of bare rock and gorges, while the eastern side is upland pasture, with many large fields, woods and huge trees in the hedgerows. This part is less well known and appreciated, except for some special pockets, such as Nunney with its ancient castle. It has its own virtues and special beauty – a hidden, secretive country without the ready access of the west.

The centre of Mendip is a maze of small lanes and upgraded tracks. One, in particular, is used increasingly by those who are travelling long distances but like to keep away from the main routes. It is quite a fast, empty road through the heart of some of the most beautiful parts of Mendip. The B3135 rises up through Cheddar Gorge, emerging to run along the top of the world and north of Priddy, over the Wells road at Green Ore, then joining the A37 at Oakhill, north of Shepton Mallet. From here a slightly circuitous road joins our favourite route of all.

Perhaps it is best to describe this from its starting place at Wells. This country road turns off the main A39, wends its way up through East Horrington to reach the highest point of Mendip before joining the A37 at a point a mile or so south of the other route. From there it runs through peaceful open countryside until it nears Frome, passing through some delightful hamlets, such as Chantry and Whatley, before entering that interesting town up a steep hill.

It is wise to beware of mist in the early morning and evening at certain times of the year, but this route is worth the effort and should not add to the journey time unless you are seduced by the countryside to stay and look a while. Returning to Wells, there is a splendid view of Glastonbury Tor framed between some branches and the church tower at East Horrington. When the light is right, the journey is worth it for that view alone.

Another spectacular road goes north from Cheddar Gorge, forking left to Charterhouse, then either left again to Burrington Combe or straight on to East and West Harptree, with views over the twin lakes of Blagdon and Chew Valley.

Not all Mendip is wild.

There are many other lanes and small roads which are worth pointing the bonnet down, just to see what emerges. We discovered the little white church at Emborough like this and some brilliant autumn colours in a wood near Chewton Mendip.

Mendip roads have few facilities other than some excellent and unusual pubs, but lead into the magic of a new world and are largely empty of traffic. What more could anyone wish?

The Main Centres

The relatively few towns or larger villages in the area act as a centre for the farming community, with schooling, libraries and other facilities for the local population. Increasingly, they have come to provide homes for commuters working in Bristol or Bath, as well as industries which give employment, although these change with take-overs and management buyouts.

In recent years most towns and some larger villages have seen new small factory units going up on the outskirts, and even farms have contributed to this with the conversion of outbuildings to craft workshops or units for very small businesses. This has helped revive the townships as well as some purely rural settings.

As we write this, local government is in the midst of another reorganisation. It appears that, in future, Mendip will be under the aegis of Somerset, instead of having part of its area in Avon, which will no longer exist. But nothing is certain until the ink is dry on the appropriate Act of Parliament.

What is certain is that the great majority wish to see a return to the old County of Somerset. Others would like to see local government move closer to their own locality, arguing that County Councils do not understand areas outside their home-base, just as many away from London feel national papers are in fact London dailies, because of the location of their management and editors. Mendip people point out that splitting the area between two authorities breaks up a natural entity and lengthens the chain rather than shortening it. Time will tell what will be the ultimate situation and effect.

There are four main centres of population on Mendip, the rest are villages and hamlets, with limited shopping and other facilities. These four range from the miniature cathedral-city of Wells to the grown-up village or small township of Cheddar, with Shepton Mallet and Axbridge somewhere in between. Although Mendip is predominantly rural, with many people living in isolation, they are important both to them and as tourist bases. They all have their roots deep in the history of the area.

The centre of ancient Axbridge is one of the jewels of the area, with its square containing attractive medieval buildings. The riches of the town, which had a regular market some nine hundred years ago, were built on the justly famous Mendip wool.

Another notable feature is the reservoir set between Axbridge and nearby Cheddar, although much more part of Axbridge when seen from Mendip above. Perhaps unjustly, this is known as Cheddar Reservoir and is home to a flourishing sailing club, as well being famous for its migrant and resident birds, some of considerable rarity.

Throughout the summer, Cheddar is packed with tourists, most of whom probably see only this aspect, concentrated as it is at the foot of the gorge. But there is much more to the town than this. Wandering along some of the roads up the hillsides to the north, it is possible to discover a wide variety of the attractive cottages and gardens of the original village.

Shepton Mallet gives the impression of a rather sad place. Although it can boast a fascinating history, somehow many areas look like a 1930s township, but without the benefits of the sophisticated shopping streets that might be expected to have followed this style.

In fairly recent times the town has been famous for two quite different establishments. Many first heard about the military prison when serving in the army. Its fearsome reputation was enough to send shivers down the neck of anyone threatened with it. Now the 'glasshouse' is no longer used for that purpose. The second is Babycham, the famous pear drink created by the Showering Brothers in the 1960s.

There ought to be much to admire in Shepton but somehow it lacks the charm of Wells of the balance of central Axbridge. This is unfortunate because it is possible that sympathetic planning could do much to restore the harmony of the centre, bringing back the hidden attraction which lies in its bones.

It is not just the Cathedral and its surrounds which enhance the city of Wells. The central area has been looked after and lovingly restored, forming a harmonious whole with the minimum of jarring modern notes. Traffic through this area is a real and growing problem, and for many years there has been talk of a by-pass. At last this appears to be going ahead and, while fierce arguments still rage over the choice of route, there is no doubt that this exceptionally lovely little city can only benefit from the peace that should ensue from this development.

Special Viewpoints

We all have our special views, secretly wishing they belonged to us alone. We leave you to make your own particular discoveries from studying the folds and intricacies of the larger scale maps – goodness knows there is enough room in Mendip for everyone without tripping over each other. However, there are some famous viewpoints which should not be missed, although they can get quite crowded.

Black Down

To visit this viewpoint involves an uphill walk; there is no way of avoiding this, but the result is well worth while. Black Down is a hill set to the north of the well-known trekking and riding centre of Tynings Farm, on the road which runs eastward from Shipham into the heart of Mendip. The view is panoramic, over the edge of Mendip to Exmoor and Steep Holm in the west, with Glastonbury Tor in the south-east, that rounded hill topped by the stark ruin of a church and dominating the surrounding moors.

One attraction of this and many other Mendip views is the constantly changing palette of colours as the clouds race overhead, bringing sunshine and shadow in quick succession. It never looks the same but always brings that sense of peace which comes with satisfaction at what is seen, a landscape which seems perfectly designed and complete. From above, unsightly detail is avoided: the incongruous modern house set among old cottages, or a rusting car tumbled into a ditch beside a field.

Cheddar Gorge

From below, look up the Gorge in the early morning, before the coaches and crowds emerge, and see it as it has stood for centuries. Gaze at the crags on the eastern side and marvel at their height and slender pinnacles.

But perhaps the finest views are obtained from the south-eastern side, reached by a narrow path in the nature reserve opposite Black Rock, well up the Gorge. The path runs south-west until it emerges over the top of Cheddar, with sweeping views across the reservoir to the Bristol Channel and beyond, looking along Wavering Down and Crook Peak. The path wanders along the edge of the Gorge before reaching this point so it is possible to look down on the cars and coaches like dots far below. There is a sense of remoteness from the realities and problems of life and the air is clean and fresh.

The awesome pinnacles of Cheddar Gorge.

Crook Peak and Wavering Down

These well-known landmarks command staggering views in virtually all directions. There are several ways up to the Peak, but the footpath is reached from the west. Park off the narrow road which runs from Axbridge and Cross to Winscombe. The view unfolds in front as the path rises, but keep going. It is worth the effort.

Draycott Sleights

This is one of the most splendid views of all, whether seen from the road descending to Draycott from Mendip top or within the Somerset Trust Reserve to the west. The road drops down, past some impressive clumps of trees on the horizon to either side, before a bend exposes the spectacular view of a curving hill framing Steep Holm and the Bristol Channel against the sweep of the Levels. Climbing to one of the higher points in the Reserve, there is a view across a magnificent line of huge trees to the great sweep of south-west Somerset, from Steep Holm to Glastonbury. It feels like the very top of the world.

Ebbor Gorge
At the entrance to the car park, pause and look south across the Levels to Glastonbury Tor, by way of a jumble of lower hills on the edge. Whether misted or on a day of crystal clarity, there is always something fresh to see. The entrance to the Gorge is on the Priddy/Wells road.

Old Holcombe
Take the road out of Holcombe and make for the Old Church, marked on the map to the north. Swing through the gate by Moore's Farm, stop and look down at the small church set in the valley below, the eye leading to it by way of the curving sweep of the field. This building is all that remains of the original village, wiped out in the Black Death centuries ago.

Leigh-on-Mendip
Leaving the old Roman road between Frome and Wells, go north to Leigh. Stop on the first corner and again on each corner beyond and marvel at the tall church tower dominating the village tucked away below in its fold in the hills. Church, village roofs and fields form a harmonious whole which it would be difficult to beat.

Pelting Drove
This is a well-known spot south of Priddy on the road to Wells, before reaching Ebbor Gorge. There is a parking area, newly planted trees and usually a good many people, but it offers some of the finest views over the green moors of the Levels, with their shining silver rhynes and the almost imperceptible hills of the Isle of Wedmore and the Poldens beyond. The view lies over the unexpected shapes of Nyland and Glastonbury Tor, rising steeply out of the flatlands, and the hills which rise nearer Wells.

The Harptrees
The road from Cheddar to Harptree leads over the top of Mendip, eventually dropping down past a little hamlet on Harptree Hill. From here, on a very steep and winding road, there are some fine views over Chew Valley Lake far below. The road from East Harptree to Chewton Mendip twists and turns its way up the scarp edge and even more spectacular views are to be obtained looking back over Chew Valley and Blagdon Lakes and the land for miles beyond.

Isolated Pubs

While it may be invidious to pick out particular pubs for comment, there is an excuse in Mendip, specialising as it does in remote hostelries away from crowds and villages, set in lonely country and exposed to all weathers. Some may have served now-vanished communities but most were there to sustain travellers and change horses when traversing the great turnpikes or coach routes by stage.

We recommend them for their location and history, rather than the virtues or otherwise of the particular brews they serve. There are many other excellent pubs in the villages and towns of the area, but these will have to be researched by the individual. Our pubs are brought to your attention because of their special nature and associations.

Castle of Comfort
An isolated inn where the roads to Priddy, Harptree and Chewton Mendip cross. The four great earthworks of the Priddy Circles are close by. This was one of the coaching inns which served the Wells to Bristol road in the eighteenth century, the others being the Hunter's Lodge, the Miner's Arms and the Wells Way Inn.

Hunter's Lodge
Is on the way to St. Cuthbert's Works from Priddy, south on the same road as the Castle of Comfort, the Old Bristol Road out of Wells. This pub is the favourite watering hole of cavers.

Mendip Inn
Situated at the crossroads where the A371, from Shepton Mallet to Bristol crosses the B3135 from Green Ore, this pub's fresh cream paint makes it far less forbidding than some of the other well-known inns on Mendip, with their dark, light-absorbing stone, grimed by the centuries. Inside the modernisers have been hard at work and it has lost much of its character.

Miners Arms
A restaurant on the top of Mendip, where the old road from Wells to Bristol crosses the Cheddar/Oakhill road. Some years ago it was one of the first to introduce snails on the menu, born and bred on their own snail farm.

Old Down Inn
Famous coaching inn on the Bristol/Wells Road, built in the seventeenth

century and notable for its gatherings of worthies in past times. It has changed its appearance dramatically at least twice in its life. Some years back the plaster, which had been applied to its walls a long time before, was ripped off and the stone is now visible. The inn was mentioned by Parson Woodforde in his journal.

Ploughboy Inn
A busy pub at Green Ore, where the fast road from Wells to Bristol is crossed by the long, straight route to Frome. It is unusual in that the interior has been opened up to a most pleasant single bar, comfortable and timeless.

Slab House
A pub set on its own high up above Wells on the B3139, north of the Horringtons. It has fresh paint and attractive gardens but looks faintly suburban, in spite of its position in the deep, rolling countryside.

Waggon & Horses: High in the mists of Mendip top.

Waggon & Horses
Perhaps the most remote of all the solitary Mendip hostelries. It stands on a Roman road which runs across the empty space above Shepton Mallet towards Frome. It is close to the Fosse Way crossing and dates from the end of the 1700s. It still has some original features, including iron diamond-panes, an outside staircase to the upper rooms, and a coach house and stables below. It is amazing to see how busy this remote inn remains even during the worst Mendip weather. Coming out into the mist you might be a hundred miles from any habitation.

Wells Way Inn
Another of the coaching inns on the Old Bristol Road out of Wells. This one is set on Harptree Hill, the incredibly steep descent down the edge of Mendip, where it joins the present A368. This has also been heavily modernised as well as extended, as old photographs show. There are remarkable views from the gardens.

The Varying Landscape

As in much of Britain, the land use continues to develop; sometimes subtly through differing levels of grazing, in other parts more noticeably with the coming of alien crops like mauve-tinted flax, tall, jagged maize and fields of yellow rape.

The EC's Common Agricultural Policy brought changes. Milk quotas and set-aside have their effect, making farmers seek to intensify production in other ways. If the natural forces of supply and demand are interfered with, they end up with continually adjusted results which are never quite right. Mendip is no better or worse affected than elsewhere by this. A good deal of the land is under permanent grass and there are still many sheep feeding on it, giving that lovely lawn-like sward which is so attractive, as well as growing a variety of wild-flowers.

The countryside is changing the whole time and will continue to do so, not always obviously for the best, but in time scars vanish and, miraculously, the peace and tranquillity of the region return. The balance remains, but it is hard to witness the longer-term effects of change knowing that what has gone will never return. For instance, the latest fashion in the western part is to set out in great fields, leaving them to root it up until it is a mass of mud. This 'ploughed up' ground is then planted with arable crops. One wild field between Cheddar Gorge and Priddy, which was covered each

Spring with carpets of bluebells and May trees heavy with creamy flowers, is currently the subject of such treatment. It is sad that this profusion will be seen no more but one has to sympathise with the farmer who has to make his living off his land.

The great upland plateaux have scale given to them by copses of large, mature trees planted long ago by our ancestors. When driving along many of the empty straight roads on the high ground, these appear regularly over the horizon, giving an impression of a gently rolling, open landscape, with sufficient trees to make it interesting.

It would be helpful at this point to describe the skeleton and surface of this countryside, starting in the west and working across towards the east, for it is considerably varied in its scale and perspective, affecting its overall appearance and the style and type of its villages.

To give an idea of how this country changes we have divided Mendip into blocks of countryside separated from each other by appearance and character, although inevitably these must be arbitrary and subjective. They are outlined on the map on p . Wandering through these will give a feel of this infinitely varied yet cohesive area of England, its beauty and its special character, recognised by so many over the centuries, from pre-history by way of the Romans, to present times. We start at the very western edge with one of its finest features.

Wavering Down

The extreme western part of Mendip, with its famous high point at Crook Peak, its few miles separated from the rest by the great valley carrying the A38. Its spectacular and instantly recognisable shape lying across the horizon makes many want to climb to the top and look down. The thin soil, with its masses of wild flowers, has white limestone erupting everywhere. Owned by the National Trust and with good access, it is a fine and spectacular location, visited by a great many people who are rarely disappointed. The pretty village of Compton Bishop nestles under the peak though is still six hundred feet above sea level.

Strawberry Country

This is the truly spectacular region of Mendip – the seamed and steeply-sloping edge which rises straight up from the sea-level plains below into the exposed rocks of the western plateau. The A361 from Weston-super-Mare to Wells winds its way along the bottom contour of the hills through a series of pretty villages which have long been famous for their market garden crops and, in particular, their strawberries, although nowadays these do not play such a major part in the local economy.

Here are found the great gorges of Cheddar and Ebbor, the caves at Wookey and Cheddar, and steep, fertile slopes which lie above the villages and towns below. The sunlit grass can be a rich vivid green, and the lovely old trees intricate and twisted. Mendip is very grand at this point, with woods sloping down into canyons. There is some plough-ground on the edge of the higher slopes, then it becomes a patchwork of smaller fields and permanent grass.

With stone walls above.

The road wanders through villages with high stone walls, and open country with farms and buildings folded into the hillside or edging the Levels down below, for this is the boundary between the flat moors and the steep limestone hillsides. And all the time the road twists and turns, slow and narrow, following the Mendip contours. The places it passes through, such as Westbury-sub-Mendip, are far larger than perceived from the road. These villages stretch up into the hills by way of a maze of tiny lanes, with cottages and houses which look as though they have grown out of the soil. These are solid, stone-built dwellings, each village varying slightly in the colour of its stone, which was dug originally in local quarries. Draycott Stone is famous for its reddish hue, while Easton houses are made from a much greyer stone. They are handsome buildings rather than pretty. There are not the fat, cob-walled, thatched cottages found further west. It seems as if they were built to withstand a harder existence, yet a relatively more affluent one.

A number of roads leave the villages and climb steeply, often in bafflingly zig-zagging directions, into the sharp edge of the plateau. If you meet anyone be prepared to back or manoeuvre for there is little room to spare. On leaving the villages there is little further sign of habitation; above a certain height the margins are without houses and the plateau above nearly as empty. The slopes are wooded in part, with copses and high-growing hedges at the bottom, and stone walls above, where the rock breaks through. One of the most attractive features is the constantly changing light and shade. Rarely does it appear the same from day to day, or from hour to hour, while some of the colours are startling in their brilliance.

One day we drove up as the snow started a slow thaw. The landscape looked sublime where the sunlight breaking through the mist gave a creamy tint to its previously blue-grey tinge. The roads were reasonably clear, but with smears of snow between the car tracks, difficult in the places where a gateway had allowed drifts across the road. The snow hung on branches, thickening the winter-bare hedges, giving it a quite different perspective – a time of magic, where the land was totally silent and little moved.

The Great Limestone Plateau

This is what many consider to be the 'typical' Mendip of the postcard and, undoubtedly, one of the main reasons for declaring this region an Area of Outstanding Natural Beauty. The visitor emerges onto the plateau from the strawberry villages below, perhaps by way of Draycott Sleights, to see a huge country with distant horizons emphasised by gently rolling fields separated by dry stone walls. Rounded copses of large trees dominate the horizon, rising up one after another as the long, straight roads unwind. It is a special area with a character of its own, quite distinct from the plateau to the east.

Across the north/south A39, at the tiny hamlet of Green Ore, stone walls become more dominant going towards Cheddar, although many have scrappy hedges on top. The old walls are extremely decayed beneath the hedges, with little or no maintenance carried out over the years, though this is likely to improve in the future, with grants available for their upkeep. Driving west, the walls lose their hedge-tops and become the characteristic dry stone walls of any limestone upland. There is some plough-ground in the distance, although most of the country is under permanent grass.

As the miles roll by, the walls become more dominant and there is a feeling of entering a completely different type of countryside. Ahead are great conifer woods which lead down to Waldegrave Pool and the Mineries. On either side of the road are strange circles, indentations and disturbed ground, a mixture of ancient earthworks and 'gruffy' ground – the mining spoil of yesteryear. These shapes and bumps are found in many locations in this part of Mendip.

Passing through the woods is like driving through the nave of a great cathedral, with the trees arching over. A winter snowfall shows up the intricate tracery of the branches, the white lightening the darkness of the fir-trees above. It is often misty up here, smudging the detail of copses and trees. As with snow, this can give a special perspective to the landscape, emphasising the graphics of hedges and stone walls snaking through the landscape.

Over the Old Wells Road crossroads there is a different land again. It is varied with the stone walls more definite, while there are signs of the limestone skeleton of the land emerging through the soil. Travelling this road in the late afternoon sun brings out the shadows behind the walls and every bump and dip of the ground is shown to advantage. There is a Military Rifle Range to the north, taking up much of the land to Charterhouse, and the red flag is often seen flying beside the road. It is now a gently rolling upland plateau, with huge trees in widely separated copses.

By turning left towards Wells, it is possible to reach another fascinating and unique region of Mendip, much loved by visitors. To one side is a car-park beside deep woods and an excellent choice of walks. On the right is the famous 'gruffy' ground of the Priddy Mineries, with Priddy Nine Barrows to the north-east and Ashen Hill Barrows in front. There is a nature reserve run by the Somerset Trust and a couple of pools much favoured by dragonflies in the summer.

Another fascinating route here begun below Shipham, turning off east by Lilypool Cider and Cheese Farm. The road runs up between steep slopes with a number of houses set high on the hillside, facing south. Horses graze the fields opposite and it is a delightful rural scene.

The road rises further, with open views across low trimmed hedges into a deep valley at the foot of Dolebury Warren, a thickly wooded slope edging Black Down. As the valley emerges into the open, the road swings left to pass Tynings Farm, a well-known riding centre. Beside it is the entrance to the footpath to the top of Black Down, with its magnificent walks and views. The fields in front of the farm give a fine perspective to the main building and huddle of stables, barns and other outbuildings which make up its sizable complex. A solid grey cottage over to the west balances and sets off the scene perfectly.

Winter landscape.

The road continues on its way, with the rough ground of the top coming down to meet the road and, to the south, the green slopes of Mendip, falling slowly out of sight below. The slender, slight-stemmed trees and bushes of the hedges lean near to the car, seeming as if they will close in and seize it. Eventually the scattered hamlet of Charterhouse appears, with its stark church looming over the dark skyline and gaunt farm buildings. From there a most interesting route follows the right turn, dropping to cross the main road by Kingsdown Farm. The last part of this hill has a wide sweeping curve of grassland bleeding straight into the road, without benefit of ditch or hedge. The road opposite climbs a hill to emerge on the top of another plateau which slopes away gently on either side, with panoramic views. Many of the trees are large, wind-twisted and intricate in their shapes, while on the horizon are pines, some of which have been knocked over like skittles in an alley. The one on the end, still upright, has its head bent over at right-angles by the wind.

This is a landscape which cries out for the detail of black and white photography on an old-fashioned plate camera. Unlike the Levels, where the search is for the intimate close-up of ditch and reeds, this scale calls for detail in the distance, the minutiae of twigs on a distant tree, the folds of the landscape and sheep dotted across far-off fields, or the pattern of stones in the walls.

North-western edge

While this is not a homogeneous whole, it does have a certain character of its own. It covers the line of villages along the softer northern and western edges of Mendip, where the hills slope more gently down to rolling country below, without that breathtaking plunge on the southern side. Facing north, these villages suffer in comparison with the strawberry slopes, the colder hillsides cutting off the sunshine earlier in the day.

A good place to start is Shipham to the west, that upland, misted village, with breathtaking views across to Weston-super-Mare, which straggles its way across the lower slopes of Mendip. This is rough, rocky country, more akin to the southern slopes than the north, but shaded and harsh. Huge quarries eat out the heart of the hill south of Shipham, and towards Cheddar, but the best view of this country is from above, while winding across to the ancient mining hamlet of Rowberrow. It is a land of steep banks with hedges on the top, giving an impression of Devon lanes. These lanes wind up and down hills with tiny grass paddocks on the northern side, and a magnificent view of Congresbury, Clevedon and Nailsea to the north-west, laid out in a great sweep below.

This is a place of cottages and farms, looking down onto Shipham village and across the edge of Mendip. Above lies Rowberrow Warren, with conifer woods much favoured by horse-riders. It is rough, steep country, with rocky outcrops and jagged horizons to the east.

There is a grand road which races across from Green Ore to the village of Chewton Mendip at the eastern end of this northern section. The road passes through a tunnel of woods at its entry to the village, then turns left down a narrow lane which leads on towards the villages at the northern fringe. With the long hill down to Chewton Mendip there is a feeling that Mendip is being left behind, but in fact it is only dropping to a lower plateau. The road runs through steep-sided fields on the right, looking over stone walls into wilder country, in contrast to some of the manicured fields encountered previously. Houses appear around each corner, and just as it seems the village has been left behind, Litton emerges, set deep in its valley beside a stream.

This side-road continues from there until it reaches the A368, the main fringe road running eastwards to Churchill. Prior to that it runs below Mendip and is not a part of it. There are steep slopes above and behind, and the traveller looks up, appreciating the great height of Mendip plateau. With a different viewpoint, the quality and shape of the country changes. A large house sits on the horizon, giving scale to the gradual long slope leading up to it. The road winds round the middle contour and then a church appears, set against a dark hill.

Over eight hundred feet near Charterhouse, on top of Mendip.

The edge of Mendip becomes much steeper by Blagdon, with some almost cliff-like falls in parts. Houses grow out of the folds in the hills, looking as if they had been there for ever. The road runs alongside stone walls and the country becomes more rolling, but it is now above the surrounding flatlands. Mendip is higher still to the left, with many trees, copses and little groups of cottages entwined in the hillside. The road leaves Burrington with one last flourish between two steep cliffs, just before Rickford, then finally abandons Mendip.

Middle Plateau

A countryside different from the western area – largely hedged, wooded and with a less spectacular feel. While there is still an echo of limestone, with dry stone walls to the west and north, it is more conventional, but with a secret air to it. The western plateau is wide-open country, with many views over to the edges, unobstructed to an open horizon. In this part views may be wide in one place but they can change rapidly to narrow prospects cut off by trees and high hedges. Some parts are full of tiny fields behind steep banks or hidden from view above sunken lanes.

From Green Ore to Burnt Wood crossroads there is a magnificent landscape, with great lines of trees on the horizon and tall hedges with mature trees standing among them. Distant farmhouses look small in this vastness, marked by great piles of black hay bales. The road is straight and long, of Roman origin. Walls and low hedges line it, although they cannot make up their minds which they are at this point, while sheep dot the fields, as might be expected in this famous wool country.

It is worth stopping at Burnt Wood crossroads to look up at the two great tumuli on the horizon to the north. They seem more like piles of spoil at first, but when it snows the dark ground shows through, in contrast to the smooth sheets of white on the fields. A line of trees runs up in a long tapering mass over the hill and down towards the road, giving a majestic sweep to the landscape. What an amazing revelation this countryside is when snow and low afternoon light bring out the intricate shapes, hollows, curls and curves of the land.

The area to the north and east of this road is quite distinct. This is mining country and the villages reflect this, many crowded and unattractive, with buildings of uncertain age and even more uncertain architecture, though some are certainly worth visiting. This country is more closed-in, with smaller fields and high hedges. There is plough-land mixed in with the pastures and either definite woods or fields, not copses within fields, as on the more open plateau. There are great bare, gaunt farmhouses, often with large outbuildings, looking as if they are hamlets on their own – self-contained, with no need for the outside world.

On the western edge lie the various old mining villages such as Gurney Slade, Oakhill and Chilcompton, set in closely-knit, shut-in countryside, with a mixture of stone walls and tiny fields between thick, high hedges. It is very varied and there are some fine woods, as well as gems like Emborough Lake, which has a dam across the end to stop the waters inundating the lane running beside it, even though it is completely natural. There are some lovely old banked lanes, worn down with use over the ages so they run below field level. In spring this is a wonderful place for wild flowers, making the lanes a delicate and varied picture.

Travelling north to Bath, the road cuts through a corner of the old part of Oakhill, before going on to the little hamlet of Nettlebridge. This was the starting point for the Dorset and Somerset Canal, which sadly never opened fully to traffic. It is fine, steeply rolling country, rich in trees, with some stone walls edging the fields. Horizons are narrowed as the road wanders and winds its way down the valley through green fields. The steep green slopes, with large, mature trees, hidden hollows and ripples in the pasture, show yet another side of Mendip's character.

One of our favourite routes brings us across the heart of the area, from the outskirts of Wells to Frome. After the first few miles the road straightens as it crosses spectacular countryside, with open views on either side over the spine of the eastern Mendips. On a winter morning the only problem is the frequent presence of pockets of mist, so beware! This road runs past one of the most isolated of Mendip pubs, the Waggon and Horses, complete with stables dating from the coaching era. Further on, a turn to the north leads to the upland village of Leigh-on-Mendip, set in a dip, with its splendid church tower outlined against the horizon, dominating the landscape.

Good riding country

North-east of Shepton Mallet the country changes once more – less pretty, more conventional, a working agricultural landscape with some fine large farms. Well beyond and east of the Waggon and Horses there is a lane to Downhead, a scattered hamlet with an unusual grouping round the church. The lane winds its way down a steep hill into the village, where it is as likely to see a tractor parked outside a cottage as a car. The country is gently rolling downland and hidden somewhere in it is a quarry, no longer working.

North from Leigh the road passes the almost non-existent hamlet of Soho, called after the Duke of Monmouth's London home, so it is said, which in turn was named after a hunting call much used in those days. There seems to be nothing more of it than Soho Cottage itself at the crossroads, although, as with other Somerset hamlets, there may well be more tucked away in nearby folds in the country.

From the great Abbey of Downside, set in its fold in the hills, the road rises up onto the bare plateau once more. Downside School has many of its facilities here, a pavilion and football pitches, and it is not difficult to imagine how cold the boys must be in this desolate, open spot, sparsely protected by rows of huge old trees. Further away, on lanes which run south of Stratton, the change is dramatic – wide open to start with, but well hidden by high hedges and banks. The road climbs higher and higher until it crosses the Fosse Way, when it becomes quite beautiful. Wandering round woods and copses, the views of the tree-framed valley could be taken for a glossy calendar. The hedges are tight and the fields rise and fall in folds and twists. There are many public footpaths which must be a joy to walk. It is all so intimate; always close to other villages. Oakhill, Binegar and Chilcompton appear on the signs, yet the roads seem lost in time, empty. There is a world to be explored in these folds and valleys.

Eastern Fringes

Change takes place as the edges of a great upland massif are reached. More attention is paid to shelter-belts and tree-planting; views alter and vistas open up, but in a different manner from those of the great plateaux. The view over an edge may be framed in trees or between hedges but, extending into the purple, rolling distance below, it has a quite different feel.

This region is best seen by way of a route starting in the extreme southeast at Nunney and working up towards the climax, the view of the great Abbey at Downside in the north.

A lane disappears over the edge of the hill, off the main A361 Shepton/Frome road, leading down to the pretty village of Nunney, with its ruined castle and lovely old cottages. It is an odd mixture – small, neat fields behind tidy hedges and tightly rolling countryside with woods and open fields. Yet those same hedges are white with the ugly limestone coating typical of quarry country, leaving it a ghost of its real self. Even nearby Mells has this tint in the hedges nearby, yet there are few prettier parts around.

It is difficult to determine where Mendip ends and the surrounding rolling hills start. Whatley – that straggly village with a prominent steeple on its church – is our bet. There is a subtle but perceptible hardening of the country here. It moves from the gentle Frome hills to a higher, more open, windswept landscape. Driving from Frome the road climbs, at first gently, then sweeping up to Whatley and round its twisting, lengthy village streets, to the crossroads by the church. Here the hedges are again lime-dusted and grey from the nearby quarry. There is a distinct impression of crossing a frontier at this point, moving over the crossroads and on to Chantry. The road drops, then rises steeply, coming up onto what is clearly an upland plateau – Mendip top once more.

From Chantry, the fringe country, hovering close by the edge of Mendip the whole while, follows local lanes through Vobster and the mining villages of Coleford and Holcombe until the great Abbey at Downside comes into sight at Stratton-on-the-Fosse.

The way to Vobster, that village with a delightful and mysterious name, is best taken through Leigh-on-Mendip and Soho. The road goes through sweeping countryside, some of it parkland, with great oaks growing in the middle of the fields, finally dropping down to a stream and then the mining village of Vobster, its heart located on a bend by the Inn. Park House – a lovely Queen Anne style mansion in Mells Park – is seen on the horizon. The lanes here are old-style English, following the boundaries of fields, or where they used to run. Clearly the Roman influence died out beyond the main route. Where it is possible to look through a gate set in the banked and hedged boundaries, the views are very fine. There is that feeling of being high up, but it is relatively flat country, without the folds and dramatic valleys further east. There may be stone under the base of the banks but this is laid-hedge country.

There are several roads to Stratton; the one from Leigh, through Holcombe, passes over flat country, with some attractive houses set off the road in little gatherings or hamlets, a farm and its next-door, joined-on cottage – master and servant shown in the size of each. The country starts to roll again at this point, though it still feels high and exposed. Manicured grass fields with hedges neatly trimmed lead to the Abbey on the skyline – huge and elegant, like some Wells Cathedral rising out of the hills, the building dominating all else with its position.

South-east Face

This area includes the pretty villages along the scarp which curves on from Wells, past Shepton Mallet and eastwards. Because this area is above sea level, it gives the scarp a rolling, less dramatic appearance. The villages are handsome, with plenty of fine old stone buildings, some large, but most of substance. These were born on the prosperity of wool, showing their origins in style and solidity and, in particular, the magnificence of the churches they raised.

The main road rushes from Wells to Shepton, through lovely valleys, with church spires and towers seen as each corner is rounded. From Shepton Mallet to the Nunney turn-off, it is more open country, with wide views as far as the great fort of Cley Hill to the east near Warminster. This is quarry country once again; lorries pass and re-pass, some no doubt attached to Merehead, operated by Foster Yeoman, with Union Jack flying and manicured lawns, an enormous gash cut deep into the countryside but landscaped and tidy. From here stone is sent all over Europe by way of a relic of the old East Somerset Railway, feeding into the national rail network at Witham.

There is some fascinating country above the village of Croscombe, reached by way of a narrow lane on an awkward S-bend to the east. The lane wanders up into a gaunt land of high hedges with a general air of dilapidation, past big unprepossessing farmhouses and grey cottages, before revealing surprising and tremendous views over to Shepton Mallet in the south-east. This is not the tourist area of Mendip known to so many, but a remote, wild spot, with uncut hedges pressing in on already narrow lanes. It is unexpected after the great open plateau of the centre and worth exploration.

One road leads into another Downside – not the village of the Abbey but a hamlet hidden in a maze of lanes on the top, some of it still being built. Towards Waterlip the country becomes softer, more intimate, with little bumps and hollows, fields small on one side but larger on the other. Mature trees grow in the hedgerows, which have been let go wild and are vaguely reminiscent of Exmoor. Some of the road is lined with ancient, tumbledown, ivy-covered stone walls, quite different in style from the bare walls of the western half of Mendip.

By Cranmore, that village famous for David Shepherd's East Somerset Railway Museum, the country changes once more to rolling downland, with copses on the tops of the knolls and some fine old oak trees. Cranmore Tower looks down from high up on Mendip edge – a folly, but very much part of this south-western fringe of the hills.

These descriptions can only act as tasters for such varied and fascinating country. When preparing this book we revisited every hamlet and village, travelling the length and breadth of Mendip to record the scenery as we went. After a while we ran out of adjectives, and came to realise how subtle are the differences between the various parts; yet they are very real. If our taster is successful, then it will lead you to make your own exploration.

Barrows and Earthworks

Mendip is richest in prehistoric relics of all kinds. It is important to realise the impact that early man had on Mendip and to list where some of the remains and relics may still be seen. Without the people who built the barrows and earthworks of the area, Mendip would not be what it is today.

Man's presence is first noted below ground in the Palaeolithic Era, where he sheltered from the rhinoceros, hyenas and other tropical wild animals which then roamed the area. The implements used were made of flint. The first traces of people living above the ground are found in the Neolithic Era, starting some 3,500 years BC, in the area between Ebbor and Priddy. This was also the time of the Long Barrows – burial chambers for the people of the time – with examples near Priddy, Chewton Mendip and Holcombe.

The Bronze Age, extending up to a few hundred years BC, brought large numbers of still-evident relics in the form of burial chambers – the Round Barrows. The numbers of these make it clear that a considerable population existed on Mendip at this time, when metal-working was being developed. The items found in these show that goods were being traded at least as far as the Mediterranean, while the bronze implements demonstrate artistic skills of a high order. Towards the end of this age the first traces of the use of lead were seen, soon to be important under the Romans and forming a vital thread throughout the history of Mendip.

The Iron Age, the flowering of technology as it was known for many centuries, brought with it hill-top camps, enormous structures with ramparts and ditches, where whole tribes defended themselves and lived a communal existence. They played a vital part in the history of this area, though not a great deal is known about them.

Thus, no history of Mendip is complete without considering the ages represented now only by the tumuli and earthworks still to be seen on the surface, while there is much work to be done in unravelling their function and the life of those who built or lived within them.

Black Down: has a number of Round Barrows in a group.

Burrington Camp: an Iron Age earthwork, small in comparison to others on Mendip.

Charterhouse: One of the richest sites of the area, ranging from the Bronze Age to the remains of a Roman mining settlement. Gorsey Bigbury is a Bronze Age circular enclosure over 160 feet across, while there are the remains of an Iron Age earthwork nearby. The Roman remains include an amphitheatre and some other enclosures alongside the Roman road which leads eastwards to Old Sarum. Various Roman relics found during excavations are held in Bristol Museum, including coins, tools and a mask.

Chewton Mendip: North of the village there is a Long Barrow over one hundred feet long.

Chilcompton: Blacker's Hill Camp is a large Iron Age fort overlooking Downside College, with enormous double ramparts and ditch.

Dolebury Camp: Is an Iron Age camp set above Churchill. This is one of the largest and finest in Britain, some 750 feet by 1500 feet in size, within stone walls and high ramparts. The camp was used after this time by both Roman and Saxon to defend the way into Mendip, as was the fort across the valley – Dinghurst Camp.

Green Ore: The battered remnants of a long barrow lie to the east, as well as prominent round barrows further east near Whitnell Corner.

Holcombe: A Long Barrow of over a hundred feet in length is set west of Holcombe, but it has been almost destroyed.

Maesbury: North of Shepton Mallet, on one of the highest points in Mendip at over 900', Maesbury Castle is over six acres in extent, and is surrounded by double banks, with a ditch between. A marvellous example of the scale and engineering of such a camp.

Mells: There are four camps – Wadbury, Tedbury, Newbury and Kingsdown– on the sides or nearby the River Mells where it runs down a gorge close to the village. Some of these are a mixture of Iron Age fortifications supplemented by later Roman defences, which add stone walls up to 15 feet high to complement the sides of the gorge in places.

Nettlebridge: Two caves discovered in woodland near the village were found to contain Stone and bronze Age pottery.

Pen Hill: Above Wells, another site of a rare long barrow. There are other tumuli nearby, as well as a fortified enclosure.

Priddy: The area round the village, particularly to the north-east, is thick with pre-history, as well as relics of the later mining eras. Two of these clusters are particularly worth seeing.

Priddy Nine Barrows is closest to, and overlooks, the village while there are other round barrows on nearby Ashen Hill. Priddy Circles is further away by the Miners Arms, but even more spectacular, consisting of four enclosed circles, surrounded with ditches, each of over 500 feet in diameter. They stretch over a mile of ground with a Roman road passing between them. No one knows what they represented – camps, places of religious significance or magic rituals.

There are many other tumuli in the area, as well as the remains of an Iron Age camp. A haunting phrase caught the eye in a book recently, perfectly describing the feelings engendered by, 'A place where dead men lie in their barrows on the skyline.'

Tynings Farm: The riding centre on the road from Shipham to Charterhouse where there are remains of a long barrow, as well as a group of round barrows.

Westbury Camp: North-east of the village there is a large earthwork surrounded by ditch and ramparts.

Wookey: Wookey Hole was occupied from the Stone Age on, and remains of rhinoceros, lions, bears and mammoths have been found in Hyena Cave.

Holcombe Old Church

3 Events which shaped Mendip and its People

Mendip has a very long history. It has always been one of the most important areas of Somerset, settled before the surrounding areas and vital for its ores and mining. It is fascinating to trace this history, finding out how people made their living and how the climate and countryside affected their lives. We can only give glimpses of the most important events in a book such as this; but there is much more to be found in libraries and archives.

From Prehistory to the Romans

Man has lived on Mendip since well before the Late Stone Age, pre-7000 BC, when the whole place was far warmer than now and tropical animals roamed the top. Cheddar man and his tools were found in Gough's Cave, while bones of rhinoceros, mammoths, lions and other animals were discovered in Wookey Hole and other caves. The temperatures altered quite drastically over the years, bringing mini ice-ages, flooding and variations in sea-levels. The last major change came around 400 AD when the present climate and peat growth stopped down on the Levels. By then the Somerset climate had become temperate, though some of those living on top of Mendip may doubt it at times.

Traces of huts have been found in various parts of Mendip, including Ebbor and Ubley, showing that Neolithic man lived above the ground. It seems that this age lasted from around 3500 BC, for over 1500 years, until the Bronze Age, and trees were already being felled in some numbers. These two periods left signs of intense activity on Mendip and have given us a rich heritage of barrows, or burial mounds, which can be seen over many parts, particularly in the western area. Long barrows, which are less common on Mendip, come from the Neolithic Age and are communal burial sites, while the much commoner round barrows are more recent, from the Bronze Age. These were elaborate chambers filled with ornaments, weapons and tools. Stone circles and other works of unknown purpose from this period when man started to flower under the influence of new technology, have also been unearthed.

This was the time when the digging of ore and extraction of metal started on Mendip, continuing until the early part of this century. The first real signs of surface mining occurred at the end of the Bronze Age in 600 BC, although man had already been on Mendip for many thousands of years.

The Iron Age followed, leading up to the Roman occupation in 43 AD. This was the time of the construction of the great hill-forts, with elaborate defences. During this period iron was smelted wherever the ore was present and lead mining became well established. Indeed, it is said that the Roman invasions in Europe were partly dictated by the need to take over the lead sources. Within a few years of their arrival they had 'nationalised' the industry, bringing it completely under their control.

It was not long before the Romans made their presence known on Mendip with an encampment at Dolebury Hill, while a Legion settled at Charterhouse, building a complete small town to exploit the lead. Coins and other objects showed that Romans were also present at Shepton Mallet before abandoning Britain in 410, though their influence continued for a considerable period. The final sign of their involvement came with plague which spread throughout the Empire and eventually reached this area, killing many people.

Dark Ages to the Enclosures

After the Romans left, the country descended into a time of darkness, often seen as the arrival of barbarism, but in reality the nation was shaped by this period, with its various injections of fresh blood to invigorate the genes – Saxons, Danes, Angles and others added to Celt.

We know of the arrival of the Saxons in the sixth century from the writings of Gildas. By the end of the seventh century the whole of Mendip had been visited or taken over by the Saxons and the population of Somerset was said to be over 50,000. At that same date Shepton Mallet had already acquired its name of *Sceaptun*, in honour of Mendip sheep.

Ina and Aldhelm
The great King Ina of Wessex, who brought the first real advances in the development of the country, had particular connections with Mendip.

Ina reigned from 688 to 726 and founded the bishopric of Sherborne, which included all of Somerset. The king went on to establish the church at Wells, destined later to be one of our great cathedrals, but above everything else published his set of laws, bringing a system of justice to the people. Eventually he believed he had done everything he could, resigned his kingship and went to Rome as a pilgrim. He was one of the greatest of our kings – wide-thinking and decisive, yet humble and pious.

His nephew, St. Aldhelm, also a remarkable man, was extremely human, as well as deeply pious. It was told that when he wanted to give a sermon in the market-place he would sing comic songs to attract an audience. He was trained at Doulting, on Mendip, and returned to die before being taken for burial at Malmesbury Abbey, where he was then bishop. He was much loved and the procession was one of the great events of the time.

Ina gave the living of Doulting to the Abbey at Glastonbury in memory of his nephew. Later King Alfred declared Aldhelm 'the finest of Saxon poets.' A hundred years later there is the first written reference to the *Sumorsoetas*, who gave their name to the county.

Alfred the Great

Another giant in the history of our country, who also had strong connections with Mendip, although usually associated with the Levels. He reigned in the ninth century, having a palace at Cheddar, the remains of which were dug up some years ago and are now visible in front of the Kings of Wessex School.

Alfred changed the course of history with his victory over the Danes and Treaty of Wedmore in 878. He was another deep-thinking man with a reverence for scholarship and belief in justice for his people. He employed monks and others in the writing of books to extend and record knowledge and bring it to the nation. The laws he passed were a landmark in the development of England, and his reign led to the first recognisable bringing-together of the various regions under a single leadership.

One of the first references to Mendip as a hunting ground came in the tenth century, when King Edmund was recorded as almost falling off the cliffs above Cheddar Gorge when following the chase in thick cloud. For over five-hundred years from Saxon times, Mendip Forest was known as a Royal hunting ground, frequented by kings and lords and forbidden to the ordinary citizen. The name persists.

Domesday

Just prior to the Norman invasion there were four great markets in Somerset, but these proliferated in the next two or three centuries. Amongst these were Nunney and Whatley, now tiny places buried in the countryside.

In order to clarify his conquest, in 1085 William ordered a census of the population, land and domestic animals in England. This record was extremely accurate, providing a fascinating picture of life in those times. The great book showed that there were just over 500 burgesses in the towns and another 12,000 'unfree' people in Somerset; but, more significantly, there were already 50,000 sheep. Axbridge was the only borough on Mendip with a population of less than 500.

It is interesting to compare these figures with the 50,000 population recorded four centuries earlier; perhaps there was another ranking below 'unfree'?

By the twelfth century there is written reference to Cheddar caves as one of the 'four great wonders of England.'

The Great Cathedral at Wells
One of the landmarks of life in the area came with the evolution of Wells Church into the present-day cathedral, over a period of centuries.

King Ina founded the first church and college in 705, but the bishopric of Wells was not declared until 909, when church became cathedral. It was destroyed later, as part of the struggle for power among bishops, then rebuilt and enlarged by the mid-twelfth century. However, the present building was begun at the end of the same century and finally completed over two centuries later, although it forms a wonderfully harmonious whole. The rich, pale yellow stone from Doulting quarry was used extensively in its construction, as at Glastonbury Abbey.

Mining
There are a number of references to prelates being granted mining rights in Mendip at this time. In 1189 the Bishop of Bath obtained a charter from Richard the Lionheart to mine lead, while in the early part of the next century another Bishop of Bath was granted a charter to dig lead and cut wood at Charterhouse. But by the end of that century Edward I had granted the Prior of Witham Friary the right to all lead mines in the Charterhouse area, as well as Priddy and Rowberrow, so life was a chancy business in dealing with kings.

By the middle of the fourteenth century Somerset was taxed over 600 sacks of wool, while Wells was the largest town in Somerset with more than 900 people.

The Black Death

The plague came to Somerset in 1348 and was catastrophic in its effect. In twelve months one third of the population of England died. Holcombe is reported as having had its population reduced to one person, after which the old village was abandoned and another built nearby on a breezy hilltop.

Concerned that the plague could spread through crowded alleys, Wells moved its annual fair to Priddy that year, where it has remained until this day, still a premier event in the region. A stack of sheep hurdles is kept on the village green as a sign that the fair will take place again the following year.

Sheep hurdles on Priddy Green.

Curiously, in spite of the ravages of the plague, this is also the year in which the remarkable Vicar's Close was built at Wells, said to be the finest medieval street left in Europe.

The Golden Fleece

This period marked the start of the great wool wealth in the region, when churches were built and many towns and villages attained their highest populations. The fourteenth century saw the first of two waves of foreigners coming into the area, bringing new skills and energies to transform the methods for adding value to the wool. Everyone was involved in the trade. The Bishop of Bath and Wells was reported as keeping flocks on eastern Mendip, while contemporary accounts showed shepherds in this harsh area earning 3/4d over and above annual wages of 26/8d. In 1470 it was reported that Somerset was the second largest producer of cloth in England, thanks in no small way to Mendip wool. It is interesting to note that by this time Wookey Hole was already known as a tourist attraction.

Wells was not always sweetness and light. The infamous Thomas Cromwell, responsible for the dissolution of the abbeys and monasteries as well as much cruelty to priests, was appointed Bishop of Wells in 1537.

In 1572 the Massacre of St. Bartholomew in France sent half a million Huguenots over the Channel, many coming to Shepton and other parts of Mendip. They brought a further range of skills, again improving the quality of cloth manufacture, and the area flourished as never before. At this time Somerset had the third highest population in England.

Mining was at its height, and the Blue School at Wells was founded to teach the sons of Priddy miners. But in 1607 a law was passed which forbade the issuing of further licences to mine lead because, it was said, the effects of lead on the brain had brought violence and lawlessness to the miners. In spite of this, peak production of Priddy lead occurred in the 1630s, while Mendip recorded its largest production some twenty years later. At the same time Cheddar cheese was described in contemporary writings as one of the 'best cheeses in England.'

Paper-making, also, was important, with new skills being brought in by the Huguenots. St. Cuthbert's Paper Mill at Wookey was known to exist before 1600 and continues to this day.

Mendip and the Civil War

The area was deeply involved in the conflict, largely supporting the Parliamentarian side. Indeed, right at the start of the war there was a major confrontation at Shepton. Royalists proclaimed a commission to raise forces and the local Deputy Lieutenants went to Shepton to protest, but were arrested. However, a huge gathering dissented so strongly that they were released; later, their men went on to attack the Royalists and drive them out of their headquarters at Wells. Some cathedral windows were said to have been destroyed by Puritan zealots and a shot or two hit the Bishop's Palace, but nothing too serious occurred.

Parts of Somerset backed the Royalists and Charles stayed at Mells in 1643, but was not met by its Roundhead owner. Charles's army was based at Shepton Mallet the following year but later the town was headquarters to Sir Thomas Fairfax, the great Roundhead general.

Railing at natural events – whinging in modern terms – is not just a contemporary feature; in the seventeenth century Mendip miners petitioned the Lord Protector to do something about flooding, which was preventing them from reaching the richest veins of ore.

The Pitchfork Rebellion

Although Monmouth's final defeat was on the Somerset Levels, his Rebellion affected the whole area, particularly Mendip. The Duke reached a welcoming Shepton in June 1685, followed by thousands of troops. He went on to try and capture Bristol but was harassed and turned back, returning to Shepton at the end of the month, but to a very different reception. After his defeat on Sedgemoor he fled back alone to the town, from thence to capture and eventual execution at the Tower.

Thirteen Shepton Mallet men were condemned to death, although one was pardoned. They were hanged, drawn and quartered by the Market Cross and their parts hoisted up in the town as a warning to others. Corruption existed then, as more recently, and Edward Strode, with whom the Duke stayed in his last days of freedom, paid a large fine to receive a pardon. A further six men were hanged at Wells and another six at Axbridge.

It is sobering to read that, while some 300 Monmouth supporters were killed in the battle, over 1,300 were later buried by locals, most by summary execution. A further 300 were hanged after trial, while some 800 were transported to the West Indies. But the regiment formed to guard the prisoners went on to fight with the great Duke of Marlborough – the same John Churchill who commanded troops at the Battle of Sedgemoor – and became the 1st Somersetshire Regiment in 1782.

James II, strengthened by this victory, went on to make his Declaration of Independence but the great Bishop Ken of Bath and Wells, refusing to accept his setting aside an Act of Parliament, was held in the Tower, tried at Westminster and then acquitted. This was the last time any king attempted to defy the will of Parliament in this country.

Industry

The eighteenth century brought with it considerable industry on Mendip. The clean, fast running, fast streams of the area supplied considerable power and were used for a variety of purposes. Paper-making flourished, with four mills on the Axe and others at Cheddar, as well as elsewhere, though excise duty was imposed on home-made paper in 1712, then repealed in 1860. But by then many of the mills had gone bankrupt, unable to meet competition from other more modern types of machinery. For instance, Stoke Bottom Mill closed in 1838; now there remains only the ruins of a village, formerly with over forty cottages.

The population of Shepton Mallet was 11,000 in the early eighteenth century, of whom 4,000 were in manufacturing of one kind or another. The present population is under 8,000.

Hannah More

One person had a particularly profound effect on the lives and future of many on Mendip. Hannah More was born to a Bristol schoolmaster in 1745. She and her five sisters remained unmarried, devoting their lives to a great many causes.

She was a beautiful young woman, known and admired by many famous people. In particular, she was friendly with the actor, David Garrick, and his wife; the great Dr. Johnson; William Wilberforce, who eventually outlawed the slave trade; Horace Walpole; and many others in politics, government and the church.

She was a 'Blue Stocking', one of that band of women who met and discussed writing, literature and other matters, and she wrote successful plays and books sufficient to provide her with considerable wealth from her own efforts.

With this money she eventually brought hope and change to many mining families on Mendip, where she is still remembered. This followed a visit to Cheddar by William Wilberforce in 1789, when he was appalled by the ignorance and poverty he saw, and asked her help in trying to overcome it.

She established three main schools and a number of lesser ones in Somerset. On Mendip, Cheddar and Shipham offered Sunday School for all the children of the area, as well as teaching industrial or domestic skills to village children during the week. Farmers' sons and others paid to be taught the three Rs. She also formed a number of Women's Friendly Societies which gave benefits at time of sickness or pregnancy, against a small subscription. Results were amazing. The children changed from ignorant, rough creatures, and the women, 'depraved and savage', to decent, god-fearing souls. Cheddar had 200 children coming on Sundays and nearly as many during the week. By 1800 her schools taught 3,000 children.

Hannah and her younger sister, Patty, raised money locally, making up the rest themselves, to fight prejudice. They were determined to help these poor people, particularly the lead and calamine miners. 1791 was the peak for the calamine industry and Shipham had over a hundred mines in fields and gardens throughout the village. When hard times came and the market dried up, Hannah bought up the ore from the local miners to try and provide some relief. Determined, strong in beliefs, though often ill, she lived her convictions, devoting her time and money to those far less fortunate than herself.

John Billingsley, Polymath
Lived at Ashwick-Grove near Oakhill from 1747 to 1811 and was one of those rare people with an influence far beyond his immediate circle.

John Billingsley was involved in so many enterprises and applied so much original thought as to defy the imagination. He wrote one of the most influential treatises on agriculture ever produced, which was then republished under government auspices. His *General View of the Agriculture of the County of Somerset*, was a considered critique of the methods in use at the time, giving his extensive and well-argued views on how to improve output from the land.

He went on to enclose much of Mendip, helped drain Sedgemoor and invented the double-furrow plough, a most significant contribution to agricultural efficiency. He was also a founder-member of the Bath & West Show. The money for much of this activity came from the Oakhill Brewery, which he started, and which went on to national fame.

The first Mendip enclosures took place at Cranmore in 1769, the start to taming what must have been a wild part. By 1794 John Billingsley wrote that over 13,000 acres had been enclosed – rapid progress indeed. The final 11,000 acres had been added by 1810, by which time many roads had been constructed. The turnpike came to West Harptree in 1793 and, needless to say, John Billingsley was an active member of the Committee.

But in the midst of this, much poverty still existed and the extensive rabbit warrens at Charterhouse and Ubley were badly needed to provide food. At much the same time the first strawberries were recorded as being sold from the farms of Cheddar. That great preacher, John Wesley, reached Shipham in 1792 and spoke to the miners.

From Georgian England to Modern Times

The Napoleonic Wars had considerable effect throughout the countryside – depressing the calamine trade, boosting the manufacture of weapons and taking men off to fight – but this period was also the peak of the industrial revolution. Newly developed steam-powered machines took away the business of local mills, placing it in the cities and altering England from an agricultural and commercial country to a great urban manufacturing power, heavily concentrated in the Midlands and the North. Inevitably, this had its effect on Mendip, changing Somerset from one of the more populated counties to much lower down the league.

However, some refugees from overseas also arrived here at that time. In 1814 Benedictine monks, driven out of France, bought the manor at Stratton-on-the-Fosse to start their Retreat. Eventually, this led to the building of Downside Abbey and the great Roman Catholic school.

Timeless Mendip.

Mining revives

In 1824, in the light of latest technology, a second look was taken at Charterhouse lead mines. They were reopened, with concentration on the extraction of metal from waste. Cornish experience was used in this process, involving engineers from that county. By 1860 over twenty per cent of the contents of the waste tips was recoverable, giving new life to the area.

In 1865, the Charterhouse workings alone yielded over 300 tons of lead and 1300 ounces of silver. Five years later a miner's wages were quoted as being 12 shillings a week. But by 1880 the boom was over; St. Cuthbert's Mine at Priddy, employing fifty men, was the last left working. This closed finally in 1908, due to pollution caused to Wookey Hole, ending an industry which had lasted over 2,500 years.

The Advent of Caving

In 1838 Cox's Cave was discovered at Cheddar and opened to the public. However, the drive towards modern interest in caves and caving came at the end of the century with underground explorations by Herbert Balch, who was postmaster at Wells for much of his life, as well as being the founder of Wells Museum.

One of the highlights of caving exploration came with the discovery of the skeleton of 'Cheddar Man' at Gough's Cave in 1903. This proved that man had been in the area for at least 10,000 years. Then, in 1969, a quarry above Westbury yielded signs of the most ancient human life in Britain, over 200,000 years ago.

In 1927 electric light enabled Wookey Hole to open as a commercial venture, while a few years later Wessex Cave Club started – the beginning of a popular sport on Mendip.

Strange Facts

The successful and well-known Anglo-Bavarian Brewery was built in Shepton in 1864 and closed finally in 1918, putting 500 people out of work. This was the result of the owner being saved from a rifle bullet by a flask of water hanging at his side. He vowed never to brew another pint of beer without, apparently, thinking of the consequences for all his employees.

It sounds incredible but apparently the last bull-baiting took place in Axbridge in 1880, while a whole pack of harriers was lost over Cheddar cliffs in 1895, when out hunting in a mist.

In 1930, and again in 1968, summer floods caused the river to run again down the surface of Cheddar Gorge, but it was only in the 1950s that piped water became generally available on Mendip fields for farmers.

Quarrying

Current worries are now firmly centred round the quarrying industry, which currently is extracting fifteen million tonnes of limestone per annum, with increases predicted. Will more licences be granted? Is the water-table going to stand up to the assault on it which this poses?

The Ironmaster

One very remarkable story is that of Fussell's of Mells, a firm famous throughout Victorian Britain for its tools. Unfortunately it no longer exists, having been declared bankrupt in 1880, after which it was taken over by a Worcestershire firm, with production ceasing in Somerset a year later.

The first mention of the family occurred in a Parish Register at Stoke Lane, near Mells, in 1644, but opinions vary as to when the firm bearing this name was founded. 1744 seems the most likely, when the lease for the mill was signed, giving title to James Fussell, an edge-tool maker. From then on the firm flourished and spread in the area. By 1791 they were well established in Mells and already exporting to America, as well as parts of Europe.

By the end of the century it is recorded that Fussell's offered to supply the army with 2,000 pikes a week, as their effort against the expected invasion by the French. By 1813 the firm was at its height, making scythes, billhooks, hay knives, spades, shovels and drainage tools.

An important venture at this time was the setting up and promotion of the Somerset & Dorset Canal, of which a branch was to have run from Frome to Stratton-on-the-Fosse, passing by Mells. James Fussell was a director, who designed and demonstrated a most ingenious balanced lock for this. However, capital was insufficient to sustain the costs of construction. Later, in 1813, the firm was reported as important enough to issue its own banknotes and engage in some aspects of banking.

The business continued to expand, with the opening of branch factories at Nunney, Great Elm and Chantry, providing work for a great many families in surrounding parishes, while a large house, the Chantry, was built near Little Elm. The Fussells were concerned about the affairs of the villages and their employees. James Fussell IV endowed and built a church at Chantry, designed by the eminent architect, Sir Gilbert Scott, and consecrated in 1846. A successor, James Fussell VI, built Chantry School, which offered schooling at all levels, as well as industrial training.

By 1880 the business had failed. Efforts to install modern machinery were fraught with problems and 140 years of history came to an end. The works at Mells were abandoned, disappearing into the undergrowth until, in 1974, the Bristol Industrial Archaeological Society excavated them to show the layout of this great industrial site with its worldwide connections.

The Canal that never was

An Act of Parliament of 1796 authorised the construction of a canal to link the Kennet and Avon Canal, near Bradford-on-Avon, with the Dorset Stour. From the point of view of this book, the most important branch was to run from Frome to Nettlebridge on Mendip.

The Act called for this branch to be completed first. Some parts of this imaginative scheme for linking the south Somerset coal-pits with the east, as well as feeding Fussell's ironworks with their raw materials, were built. Unfortunately, capital was exhausted by 1803, with the last mile or so not dug, and other sections still incomplete. It was supposed to be a pause for re-capitalisation but this never came about.

Barges are said to have run between Edford and Coleford, but they never managed to exploit the coalfield and earn the money needed to make it a going concern, and, with the coming of the steam railways, it became a lost cause. Practically no trace of this ambitious venture now exists, except for some remains of an ivy-covered aqueduct near Holcombe and a stone embankment near Frome.

Railways on Mendip

Mendip has had its fair share of railways – at one time Wells had three separate railway stations operating at the same time, while many of the quarries had either narrow-gauge railways or horse-drawn tramways to haul their stone to connect with the main lines. But by the 1960s, following the great closure programme instituted by Dr. Beeching, most were no longer in existence.

Railways first came to Mendip in 1858, when the Bristol & Exeter Railway opened up at Shepton, eventually running from Wells, Shepton Mallet, Doulting Siding and Cranmore to Witham. A second railway later ran through the town. The Somerset & Dorset Railway (the 'Slow & Dirty'), ran from Highbridge, across the Levels to Wells. Then there was a gap before the line continued from Shepton through Maesbury and Binegar to Bath. Wells also had a station for the Cheddar Valley Line of the Bristol & Exeter Railway, from Cheddar and then on to Yatton to join the line to Bristol. All this activity covered a span of years, with rail coming to Cheddar in 1869.

In addition to these there were the quarry tramways, later converted to narrow-gauge railways, which hauled stone to the main lines. The largest of these ran from Downhead, via Waterlip, to Cranmore, while the track between Oakhill and Binegar, built in 1904, carried Oakhill Stout through-out the country. Other private railways ran to Vobster, to Whatley and to Mells itself.

Names changed over the years as one company took over another before nationalisation in 1948, but with the closure of many branch lines in the 1960s all that is left of this once vigorous network is a private line running from the giant Foster Yeoman works at Merehead Quarry to join the main line at Witham, which runs from Exeter and east to Reading and Padding-ton.

Although perhaps not quite all, for David Shepherd, the well known wildlife artist and train enthusiast, has opened up a new East Somerset Rail-way, by way of a charity under this name, running steam trains from Cran-more for a short distance towards Shepton Mallet. The old engine sheds at East Cranmore now hold a steam railway museum under the same aus-pices, a mecca for enthusiasts.

4 Towns, Villages and Hamlets

Mendip is not a highly populated area, for much of it is bleak, wet and, to use a modern term, not particularly user-friendly in winter. The larger towns and villages are situated round the southern edge, where they are sheltered, have a better climate and are on, or close to, fertile market garden soils. Others used to be a part of the wool processing industry based round Mendip sheep.

There are some larger villages in the interior but they tend to be associated with mining or quarrying, both industries which were prodigal of labour. Before the days of rapid, cheap transport, those people had to live close to their work and hence the evolution of places like Coleford or Holcombe.

Nonetheless, there are many fascinating and delightful places to visit on Mendip, from the glory of the centre of Axbridge to the subtle attraction of an old hamlet like Leighton, with its original buildings huddled together as they have been for centuries. While not every tiny hamlet is mentioned, we have attempted to cover the great majority. For any which have been left out, please accept our apologies.

The sections that follow do not form a gazetteer of the area but are easier to follow when put into alphabetical order, with the four largest claiming rank and taking precedence. From the information gathered we have had to be selective and leave out much about these fascinating and ancient places. We have attempted to give at least a feel and a taste of the style, character and present appearance of each, as well as its history.

Churches are mentioned frequently because they formed the heart of many villages, often being raised on the strength of riches made from local wool. Some of these represent the finest buildings in England and the area is noted for their richness, superb proportions and glory.

At the end of the fourteenth century Somerset was said to produce more than a quarter of all wool in England, with Wells, Bath and Frome as the centres and others at Mells and Croscombe; hence the riches of the area and the spate of church building of the Perpendicular period, for which Somerset is famed. It is worth reflecting on the values placed on these buildings when they were built, and their size in relation to the population. They were the vision in stone of a deep religious belief and their towers soared up towards God, who was a living being to those who built them.

The Townships

Axbridge

Axbridge, the only borough on Mendip in Saxon times, was a market town, with Mayor and Corporation, from the reign of Henry VIII to the late nineteenth century. There has been little new building in the centre, which remains an unexpected gem, and the bypass has served to prevent the destruction which has occurred elsewhere in places with winding medieval streets. Although there are extensive new estates on the southern side, these are not intrusive. It has a current population of just under 2,000 people.

The heart of Axbridge is the square, overlooked by the church which is reached by a flight of Draycott stone steps. On the west side is a splendidly restored merchant's house dating from the fifteenth century. Its elegant black timber framing, white plasterwork and overhanging upper storeys both dominate and complement the other fine buildings round the square, now turned into shops, a bank and restaurants. It is known as King John's Hunting Lodge, although it was not built when he visited the Royal Forest of Mendip. In fact, it is a well preserved Elizabethan merchant's house, restored by the National Trust and housing a museum which is well worth a visit.

There is a Regency town hall, within which are found the Royal Charters, silver maces from 1623, the ale-taster's glass and branding irons for cattle from the area. Further up High Street is the Manor House of Axbridge.

The church of St. John the Baptist is of the Perpendicular period, from the fifteenth century. Notable features include a Jacobean plaster nave roof and fifteenth century font, as well as a fifteenth century painting of Christ. Church treasures include ancient chalices and patens, as well as an altar covering made in the eighteenth century by the squire's wife, which is said to be one of the finest in England.

The town has a long and well-recorded history, going as far back as the Romans. A royal possession, it was used as a resting place for hunting parties in Mendip Forest in Saxon and Norman times. Edward I granted a

Charter for a Fair on St. Barnabas Day to the Bishop of Bath & Wells. In the nineteenth century Petty Sessions were held in the Town Hall every Saturday, and there were also a Saturday market and two annual Fairs at that time. Every September Axbridge holds its popular Blackberry Fair, keeping the tradition to this day.

It is a pleasant small town which slumbers in the sun beneath the slopes and is well worth exploring. There is none of the sense of rush and bustle associated with the hard-sell of Cheddar Gorge, but rather a relaxed air of comfortable, continuing life, which goes on regardless of visitors. There is a welcome to all and the small streets and alleys beckon to the adventurous.

King John's Hunting Lodge, Axbridge Square.

Cheddar

The original name probably came from the Celtic words for 'cliff' and 'water', both of which are plentiful. The village was the centre for the Royal Forest of Mendip, a hunting reserve, and at Domesday was still owned by the Crown, being split up later. Nowadays, it is difficult to decide whether Cheddar is a large village or a small town, with its 1993 population of over 4,000 people, who choose either to live in the old original cottages up on the hill, or on one of the new growing estates out below.

Cheddar beckons to the crowds of tourists who come to look at the Gorge, sample the many delights of the caves and shops, and climb the 322 steps of Jacob's Ladder. Cutting one and a half miles into the face of Mendip and with a vertical height of 500 feet on the southern side, it is easy to see why it has long been described as the most magnificent limestone gorge in the British Isles. It has been formed by the waters of the stream cutting and dissolving their way down through the rocks in the Pleistocene period more than one million years ago. Since then the surface has remained dry, though twice this century it has flooded in bad weather. The water surfaces in the village as the River Yeo, with a normal output of 15 million gallons a day, although this more than quadruples at times. Indeed, in the eighteenth century some fifteen water-mills were located in this area.

The ancestors of the present Lord Bath obtained the manor of Cheddar in the sixteenth century and have retained an interest ever since, owning and running the caves and other attractions in the Gorge. Gough's Cave was occupied during the Ice Age, Iron Age and Roman times, and the remains of mammals found in lower levels include such exotica as Mammoth, Bison, Hyena and Cave Lions. The caves have yielded interesting examples of Roman pottery and coins, and were known to visitors as early as the

twelfth century.

The first reference to Cheddar came in the will of Alfred the Great. In Saxon times the Kings of England retained a Royal Palace there, the remains of which may be seen in the grounds of Kings of Wessex School, a large, modern comprehensive drawing in pupils from a wide catchment area. This is a far cry from the school for the poor established by the eighteenth century benefactress, Hannah More, whose cottage may still be seen in the village.

Not far from an excellent example of a medieval market cross in the centre of the village is St. Andrew's Church, which was

Peaceful carving, St. Andrew's Church.

important as a minster before the Conquest. Built of red Draycott stone, its 110 foot tower rises high over the surrounding moors. It has an elegant, colourful interior and contains the tomb of Sir Thomas Cheddar, a merchant who died in the fifteenth century. There is stained glass of that period, as well as some sixteenth century treasures. Gargoyles keep watch at the front of the building, while the back is largely unornamented, except for the beautiful pierced parapet to the roof on both inner and outer walls. Together with the attractive St. Andrews House and Vicarage next door, it forms a peaceful enclave of old Cheddar, only feet away from a busy corner of the main road.

Cheddar is famous for its cheeses, of which some is still made locally, although it has become a worldwide product. Cheddar Cheese was well known as early as the thirteenth century, and 400 years later was described as the 'best in England.' In the eighteenth century the village became famous for its strawberries and justly remains so, although foreign imports have led to a dramatic decline from the days when they were rushed by the Strawberry Express to London and Birmingham markets as soon as they were ready. As a result of Dr. Beeching's axe in September 1963, the ninety-four year old Cheddar Valley Line was extinguished, though the area remains noted for its market garden crops and a vineyard.

Local industry, too, is growing, with the recent construction of an industrial estate, but, apart from commuting to such places as Bristol, the mainstay of the Cheddar area is quarrying. There are several quarries based nearby, on Shipham Hill and the slopes of Cheddar itself, employing a great many local people. Controversy may exist about the present rate of extraction from the Hills, but nonetheless a great many families depend on it for their livelihood. They are not heard complaining about mess, giant lorries or pollution from dust and lime-burning.

Shepton Mallet
This ancient town huddles under the folds of the Mendips, alongside the River Sheppey flowing from nearby St. Aldhelm's Well, which stream once worked many mills in the era of prosperity from the wool trade.

The town has as long and honourable a history as any in the region but, unfortunately, this is not very obvious from a brief look today. In the Middle Ages it was one of the most prosperous towns in Somerset, rich on the wool trade, with fine houses and a large population which gave way to none in pride in their success and township.

Now much of the ancient heart of the place has been taken apart, to be replaced with a controversial shopping centre of bare concrete and high-rise blocks of flats. However, do not leave it out of any schedule. The old roots still exist and the history is remarkable, particularly through its key location. From Roman times Shepton Mallet has been important for its position on the Fosse Way, which ran through nearby Cannard's Grave. The name reflects its centuries-old interests – *Sceaptun*, or Sheeptown, is derived from Saxon words meaning a sheep enclosure.

The town centre is built on a hill and an ancient Market Cross lies at the heart, while the remnants of five-hundred year old wooden shambles, or market stalls, are preserved nearby. The pinnacle of the cross was carved in 1500, but rebuilt in 1841, with eighteenth century arches surrounding it. There are splendid views from the Market Place with its streets running downhill. The town has its Museum, as well as an art and cultural Centre. A Fair, dating from 1235, is still held each August.

The Showering brothers created their famous pear drink, Babycham, in the 1960s. The family had been cider-makers and brewers for generations and, by clever marketing and television advertising, introduced this new taste, which soon became a national favourite. Some years later, when the firm was taken over by giant Allied Breweries, Francis received due recognition as chairman of the whole organisation. More recently, management bought out the Babycham name and production facility, giving it a new, independent life of its own, which has now passed to a Bristol Head Office.

The history of the place is fascinating and lengthy. A Roman house and relics were found during railway excavations in the middle of the last century, while a charter dating from 705 AD is kept in Taunton Museum. Given by King Ina and witnessed by the Archbishop of Canterbury, it granted lands to Abbot Berwald of Glastonbury Abbey.

A tale originating from this same time is worth recounting – whether there is any truth in it, no-one knows. St. Indractus, son of an Irish King, was on a journey to visit the tomb of St. Patrick at Glastonbury. He and his companions had brass-tipped staves and carried wallets filled with seeds which they were taking back to Ireland. Unfortunately, some of King Ina's men thought they were carrying gold and murdered them, hiding the bodies in a deep pit, but a pillar of light illuminated the spot and the bodies were discovered. The King then had the saint buried in a stone tomb, but it is not said what happened to the murderers.

Shepton was passed to a Norman knight at the time of the Conquest, but remained under control of the Abbots. The Manor of Shepton was described in detail in the Domesday Book as consisting of '5 homesteads, 7 villeins, 14 Borderers and 6 Serfs'. In addition there was 'a mill, 38 acres of meadow and 3 square furlongs of pasture'.

It then passed into the hands of the Malet family in 1100, who added their name to that of the town. The Shepton Estate managed to stay in Malet hands until 1337, when it reverted to the State. After various other changes, eventually it became a part of the Duchy of Cornwall.

In the fourteenth century many French, Dutch and Belgians came over after the Black Death. They helped change the cloth industry, improving quality and turning it into a flourishing export trade. Then the Black Death started in 1348, sweeping away one third of the population of England in twelve months. This followed earlier famines which had already had great effect and the population of Shepton was reduced to less than three-hundred, although it rose again to 425 by 1377.

In the mid-sixteenth century a further wave of Frenchmen came to the area, following the massacre of the Huguenots. As a result of this influx of talent and knowledge, there was another boost to the West Country wool trade in which Shepton was a prominent player. Many factories were built to manufacture cloth, tools and other products. These led to cottages and larger houses being built, in times of unparalleled prosperity for the town.

But all was not light. In 1535 the last Roman Catholic priest of Shepton Mallet was hanged in the Market Place for refusing to recognise King Henry as head of the church at the end of the seventeenth century, while Jane Brooks, condemned as a witch, was executed.

During the Civil War Shepton was a prime player and there was a time when all eyes were on the events unfolding there. On 1 August, 1642, at the very start of the War, the Marquess of Hertford, who was billeted at Wells, issued a 'Commission of Array' to raise forces for the King. The Deputy Lieutenants declared their support for Parliament and were arrested in Shepton, but the crowds were so large in their support that they were released.

Then came the great 'Pitchfork' Rebellion. In June 1685 the Duke of Monmouth reached Shepton after landing at Lyme Regis and was welcomed by the town, many people joining him. It was not long before he was back in the area after his defeat at Sedgemoor. Later, twelve men were executed by the Market Cross, bringing the Rebellion to an end.

The Bath & West Show was founded here in 1777, continuing to this day on a permanent site nearby. In the eighteenth century the population was said to be 11,000, with over 4,000 employed in the various factories. By contrast the population in 1801 was 5,100 and in 1981, 6,300, although this had risen to over 7,800 by 1993.

But for all the earlier apparent prosperity, there was plenty of trouble later, with Corn Law riots recorded in 1746, 1748, 1749, and in 1775, continuing to rumble on into the first quarter of the next century.

Many factories closed because of the workers' opposition to change, and Shepton went into decline, with considerable unemployment. However, some relief came with the opening of local silk mills and through brewing. In 1864 a brewery was built which continued as the Anglo Bavarian Company until 1918.

In 1855 the first meeting was held in Shepton to propose the building of the East Somerset Railway, of which Brunel was the company engineer. The station opened in 1862 and the last train ran in 1963, a sad end to this great era.

A Saxon church was known to exist before the Conquest but this has vanished completely. Now there is the church of St. Peter and St. Paul, with a fourteenth century tower, and one of the most magnificent waggon-roofs in England, supported by thirty-six carved angels. There are 350 panels and 300 bosses in this roof, each of which differs from the next. Some parts of the interior date from the early 1200s but, as with many of our churches, some was rebuilt in the nineteenth century. However, the eastern end of the nave is Norman. Church treasures include chalices and flagons dating from the sixteenth century. There are two fine seventeenth century effigies of knights, one of whom, William Strode, has his whole family kneeling by him.

But, crammed into the side of the raw concrete of the new centre, the church is curiously disappointing from the outside, in spite of the praises heaped on it.

Wells

Once among the largest towns in the country, it is now the smallest city. It has retained its medieval atmosphere without being taken over or spoiled by new buildings.

Any look at this beautiful and universally admired city must start with its great and glorious cathedral.

King Ina founded a church here in 705 and the first cathedral was built in 909. A Norman replacement for this completely vanished Saxon church was consecrated in 1148, while the present cathedral was begun by the Normans in the twelfth century and completed some 250 years later. This cathedral-church is one of the most remarkable and satisfying buildings in Britain, being described as 'the crown of Somerset'. Pevsner, in a rare display of emotion, described the builders achieving a new style which he said 'represents the most original treatment of space in architecture of which any country at that time was capable.'

The cathedral was built in two intense periods of work over sixty years from 1180, and another fifty years culminating in 1340, although it was consecrated in 1239. Various chapels and other buildings, including the Chapter House, were added between the end of the thirteenth century and half way through the next. In the mid-fourteenth century, strains were found in the structure which was starting to move, and the famous 'scissor' or strainer arches were added. Some people believe these detract from the appearance, but we feel they are the crowning touch to the whole structure, a great expression of space and freedom. Without these Wells would be a fine cathedral, with them it reaches the ultimate expression of architectural grace.

The West Front of the Cathedral is perhaps the best known feature, with its four-hundred statues sculpted in the thirteenth century and recently restored with great skill and sympathy. It was the first time such an outdoor glory of sculptures had been displayed in England.

On the north face of the tower is another of the cathedral's great treasures. Jack Blandiver and his clock have been set in the side for over 500 years. Every quarter of an hour he kicks his heels to start two armoured knights striking the bells with their battle-axes outside the walls. At the same time mounted knights run around the wall in the transept below. This clock was constructed in 1390, though the workings have been replaced since then, to the original designs. The old works are in the Science Museum in South Kensington and still continue to operate. The dial is over six feet wide, though this is not always realised by the many fascinated visitors from all parts of the world who watch it in action.

The Chapter House is one of the most inspiring and beautiful buildings of this type in England. A series of heavily worn steps curl up into the entrance, going on into the Chain Bridge. On entering the Chapter House the eye is met by 36 stone ribs rising up from pillars on the sides, to meet above and drop down from the ceiling in a column of the most glorious tracery of stone. The building is octagonal, light and airy, with ornate windows in each section.

The Chain Bridge over the Chain Gate was built to provide a covered way to the Vicars' Hall, which leads into medieval Vicars' Close. On the opposite side of the cathedral lie the cloisters, a huge open area with music rooms and a chained library built over the top. The cathedral close and precincts were largely finished in the fourteenth century, although work continued on individual buildings over the centuries.

The Bishop's Palace is equally beautiful. Off to one side of the cathedral, it is reached through a great stone fourteenth century gatehouse, the Bishop's Eye, revealing cool green lawns surrounding a moated building. Waterfowl dot the surface and there is an old tradition of swans ringing a bell when they want to be fed. The eight-hundred year old Palace is reached over a drawbridge. Originally built by Bishop Thomas Bekynton, it was restored in the nineteenth century, lending it a more romantic air than the original. The moat is fed by springs which rise nearby and give the city its name.

Wells Cathedral and Bishop's Palace.

The Green is reached from the Market Place by way of fourteenth century Penniless Porch, and the view is northwards to a handsome row of stone buildings, on the far side of a lane edging the Green. One of the most extraordinary relicts in Europe is to be found off this, a remarkably well-preserved fourteenth century cobbled street, reached through an arch beside the Chain Gate. Vicars' Close is over 450 feet long and was built with a subtle decrease in width as it runs to the north, giving an exaggerated perspective which adds greatly to its attraction. Each house has tall chimneys which increase the effect further. The street was built as dwellings for the college of Vicars Choral but some have now been taken over by the music scholars of the Cathedral School. It has a timeless air which even the most outrageous modern clothing does nothing to offset.

Other notable buildings include a fifteenth century Deanery and a Tudor Chancellor's House, which has been turned into a most fascinating museum, though in appearance it is more akin to its eighteenth century rebuild. Within the museum may be found relics from Mendip caves, pigs of Roman lead found near Charterhouse and, as important as anything else, a library of local papers and books. The much-altered ancient original Archdeaconry has been turned into a library for the Theological College.

The Market Place has a fine, austere, late Georgian town hall, with later additions, and the former Market House, dating from the early 1800s, which now holds the Post Office. The Town Hall still has a letter from Charles I, requesting money for his cause. There are a number of old inns and hotels in the city, including the King's Head, with its fine fifteenth century roof, the seventeenth century Crown, and the Swan with fittings from that period.

Two further groups of buildings are worthy of attention. The Old Almshouses were founded by Bishop Bubwith in 1436, and have a medieval Hall attached to them containing an ancient chest. Priests' Row is a handsome street running across the city, with a number of well-preserved old houses. The attraction lies in their variety.

Wells had a station on the East Somerset Railway, which opened in 1862, with the last train running in 1963. In fact, the city had three railway stations for a few years in Victorian times, but amalgamation and competition soon reduced these. Currently, there is a population of over 10,000 people with an interesting mix of industry in the city, from baby foods and defence projects to a company manufacturing many of the trolleys used in supermarkets throughout the country.

St. Cuthbert's, the largest parish church in Somerset, is often mistaken from afar for the cathedral. Its 122 feet tower commands the western end of the city and is particularly bright following a recent clean. It is built of the same creamy Doulting stone as the cathedral and has an interior which stands up to the impressive exterior. It was built in the fifteenth century, with some earlier thirteenth century parts still surviving. The fifteenth century pulpit has some fine carving and there are a number of ancient treasures, including a sixteenth century chalice, seventeenth century paten and later chalices and salvers.

Villages and Hamlets

Ashwick

The name is Saxon, so this village is a great deal older than it appears. It is set near Oakhill, almost a part of that village, on the northern top of Mendip and is one of those curious Somerset hamlets which are a puzzle as to where you enter and leave. The village is small and widely spread, the signs to it soon petering out. For all that, some earlier descriptions were derogatory because it is an attractive little place, folded into curves in the ground.

Nearby Ashwick Grove was home to John Billingsley from 1747 to 1811. The house was demolished recently.

The church of St. James was refurbished and rebuilt in the nineteenth century, but the Perpendicular tower was left as it was, the whole tucked away in deep country. Ashwick Court, the big house, dates from 1700 and other smaller houses also appear old. A quiet, understated village in deeply rural surrounds.

Binegar

A small village over 750 feet up in central Mendip, often shrouded in cloud. It is a mixture of rather uninteresting, modern or pre-war housing, with a curiously attractive area remaining round the green, with one or two fine old houses. Looking at it now it is difficult to imagine its long history, with the name being noted as Beazenhangra as far back as the eleventh century.

Quarrying was once extensive, but now only one quarry is left. Like Priddy, the village had a Fair transferred from Wells at the time of the Black Death, although it did not survive after 1955. In the eighteenth century it was a four-day event over Whitsun and was famed for its horses, brawling and bare-knuckle fights.

Its station, once an important part of the Somerset and Dorset Line, was closed in 1966. It fed over 2,000 barrels a day of Oakhill Brewery's famous Stout, by way of a narrow gauge line from Oakhill to the outside world, as well as stone and coal. However, the first war killed the brewery business and it closed shortly after.

Binegar has a large church famous for its very fine statuary on the tower, a fourteenth century image of the Holy Trinity. But the square tower is the only remains of this church, the rest being rebuilt by the Victorians.

Blagdon

An attractive village built of red stone set on the northern slopes of Mendip, with steep hills on one side and views over lakes below. What is so pleasant about these older villages are the different angles of the houses, one from another; only occasionally do they stand in rows and then are designed to form a harmonious whole. The road winds through the heart of the village, with its many fine old houses, but there are lanes shooting off both up and down hill. The numerous stone walls add greatly to the character of the place. The road from Burrington to Blagdon is particularly beautiful.

It remains a village favoured by commuters to Bristol in spite of the fact that the direct railway line to Bedminster has now been closed. Perhaps unexpectedly, Blagdon is also connected with Mendip minerals and ores. It is recorded that a lead mine which existed here in 1609 was the subject of a raid by other owners in an attempt to close it down, presumably to raise the price of their product. It was also the location of another one of Hannah More's schools, started at the end of the eighteenth century. The village must have had its fair share of 'ignorance and poverty' at that time for her to deem it worthy of attention.

The red sandstone church of St. Andrew sits on a promontory to the south of the village in a splendid position. It must be agreeable to emerge from it on a Sunday morning and look over the lake down below, which is fed by the Blagdon Yeo. The church has a Perpendicular tower over 116 feet high, but the rest was completely and sympathetically rebuilt in 1907 by a member of the Wills tobacco family.

Burrington

Best known for its Combe rather than the quiet village off to one side. The Combe is a splendid gorge second only to that at Cheddar, but set on the north side of Mendip. Beacon Batch, at 1,066 feet the highest point on Mendip, lies just above. The Combe contains eighteen known caves and potholes and is much used for both caving and rock-climbing, as well as rambling and picnicking.

The village is reached by a separate road and is a quiet, attractive little place built largely on a long straight lane which rises up into the hill beyond the church, before going east. It is curiously reminiscent of parts of Shipham, though without the mess of telegraph poles and wires.

The history of Burrington is as old as any. One of the caves in the Combe was found to hold fifty Stone Age skeletons, while Dolebury Camp above the gorge is an Iron Age earthwork. Calamine was worked at Burrington during the end of the seventeenth century. In the eighteenth century, the Reverend Augustus Toplady composed the hymn 'Rock of Ages, after sheltering from a storm in the Combe. In the early part of this century the Combe was closed to traffic during August Bank Holiday for church services held in the open, such were the numbers of people taking part.

Holy Trinity is an interesting and intimate church, set in the main street in an unusual churchyard. The building dates from the fifteenth century and is ornamented on the outside with some fine gargoyles. The square tower is mellow with age, its external bulge marking the line of the inside staircase, but the remainder looks as if it had been modernised with less sympathy, though the proportions are good. Nevertheless, it forms a pleasing whole and there is a fine roof inside, while some ancient fragments of fifteenth century glass remain.

Burrington Combe, climbers under instruction.

Chantry

A little hamlet set near the top of Mendip, reached after rising up from Frome in the east. The country changes considerably as the road steepens, becoming a plateau with huge views. It is the gateway to Mendip proper.

The village lies in a cleft in the hills and is spread out, with a mixture of pretty cottages, some larger old houses and fine walled gardens. It is interesting that the 1:25,000 map shows the village in two parts, with the scattered houses on the Frome side followed by a gap, then a former pub and group of stone buildings on the corner. However, the old one-inch map shows the second part as a separate hamlet, Little Elm.

Chantry became better known in the nineteenth century through its connection with James Fussell, the ironmaster. He built his mansion nearby, with its carefully laid out grounds, and then went on to erect a school and church for the village. Holy Trinity Church is really only notable for its design by the great Victorian architect, Sir Gilbert Scott.

Chantry is one of the few, and fortunate, 'Thankful' villages to which all the men returned after the Great War.

Charterhouse-on-Mendip

A high, remote and scattered hamlet on eastern Mendip, with many ancient remnants nearby, from the Bronze Age and Roman era. There is much gruffy ground with the remains of filled-in mine shafts. The village is at the centre of the old mining area and is set over a thousand feet up on a particularly wind-swept part. Nearby GB Cavern is famous for its bat population and huge chamber over 120 feet long with an awe-inspiring roof, but is not open to the public.

There are some large farms with big barns, and an unusual-looking house which holds the Charterhouse Outdoor Education Centre and the Mendip Wardening Service. At the time of writing, this place had been much in the news, heavy losses leading to a rethink about its work, to see how it can be made to pay for itself. It would be a pity if it was forced to close as it provides young people with a fine introduction to this fascinating countryside.

The most notable feature of the village is the extraordinary-looking church. It stands against the always varying sky, dominating the area. Its short wooden spire and buttressed walls are best seen as evening is falling, silhouetted against the sunset. Although it looks so much a part of the landscape, it was actually built in this century. Inside it is unusual in that it has fireplaces, a sink and a copper, reflecting the climate and lonely nature of the place.

The area has a long history of occupation by man, in spite of its inhospi-

73

table nature. There are several remains of ancient sites, including Gorsey Bigbury, a huge Bronze Age enclosure, and an Iron Age earthwork. There was an extensive Roman lead and silver industry, while the remains of a Roman amphitheatre lie nearby. Some finds from these, including coins, gems, mining tools and a bronze mask, may be seen in Bristol Museum.

Witham Friary, which owned Charterhouse, was one of a number of establishments started as acts of reparation for the murder of Thomas à Becket. There has been a farm here since those days, probably worked by lay brothers originally. The Carthusians kept large flocks of sheep and are said to have been responsible for developing the distinctive Mendip breed. In the seventeenth century a large house was built on the site of the present Manor House. One of its owners was created Baron Mendip in 1799, a descendant still sitting in the House of Lords. But now Charterhouse is just a lonely hamlet, reflecting the disappearance of its mainstay, the great mining industry of Mendip.

Chewton Mendip

A pretty and rather stately village on the old stage coach route between Bristol and Wells. Nearby is the source of the river which feeds Chew Valley lake down below.

The Manor of Chewton, one of the four Lords Royal of Mendip, has been in the Waldegrave family for many centuries, although they have lived there a much shorter time. Cheese is still manufactured in the village, but the formerly strong lead mining industry has long ceased. The village was known as Ciwetune in the ninth century.

The entrance to the village is down a dark tunnel of overhanging woods between stone walls, then sunlight and old houses burst into view. But much of it is off the main road, winding down towards Litton in an almost continuous flow of old houses with fine cottage gardens. Steep hills drop down to the houses, giving it a tranquil and attractive prospect.

A narrow lane off the main road leads up to the Church of St. Mary Magdalene. The impressive tower, at 126 feet the tallest on Mendip, is framed among a froth of leaves from some huge trees. The church is Perpendicular, but some Norman parts remain. A number of the windows have long been closed off, making the interior eerily dark since the only light percolates through rich stained glass. Some fragments of fifteenth century stained glass still remain. Inside there is an ancient stone seat believed to be one of the very few 'frid' stools in the country – a seat of refuge for those claiming sanctuary.

Chilcompton

A village of great variation between pretty old areas and raw, new buildings in unattractive settings. There is both industry and housing here, with old and new seeming to be almost parts of different places. The centre is off the main road and a stream runs down the side of the principal street. Mulberry, the well-known maker of bags and other products, has its modern factory hidden behind banks on the main road, as befits a company which prides itself on quality.

The name Chilcompton is said to come from ancient words meaning the 'cold valley village', and it is best seen from above, off the Fosse Way past Norton Hall, down a steep, narrow lane with tall hedges shading in on both sides until, rounding a corner, what seems to be a great abbey appears below, beside and a part of a group of solid, very old farm buildings.

This is no abbey, but the substantial church of St. John, heavily rebuilt in 1897. It looks compelling from a distance but has less character close to, while the inside is modern and plain, with little to recommend it other than its size. A well-designed stone church hall has been added recently, joined to the church by a closed wooden walkway. A huge yew in the churchyard is believed to have been a sapling at the time of Agincourt.

Next door Manor Farm, with its surrounding cottages and buildings, is large, now split into separate houses but still with the coherence of the old family farm. Beyond the church lies the Manor House, built in the early 1600s with mullioned windows, mellowed with age. The stone is of that type so often found in mining villages, black with age and grime but pale, with flecks of red sandstone in it, when newly cleaned. Many of the cottages are attractive and the older parts give the impression of a comfortable old village which has stood there for a long while, becoming used to its surrounds and itself.

Coleford

The name of this north Mendip village is derived from the presence of both water and coal. A coal pit with coking ovens existed until the end of the last century, but there are few signs left now.

Although it is freshly painted, neat and tidy, exuding an air of well-being, there is little to attract the visitor. It is one of the longest villages in the area, extending along the main street for a mile. There is an old heart with a small green and some typical mining village houses, but much new development at the eastern end with a hotch-potch of houses from throughout this century and earlier. A large British Legion hall is a tribute to the size of the place.

Surface coal digging is recorded from as early as the fourteenth century but the village's principal fame now lies in the remains of the uncompleted Dorset & Somerset Canal. Coleford viaduct was the most significant of the finished works on this project, which was designed to link Frome and Stratton-on-Fosse for the transport of coal and products of Fussell's Iron Works. A number of lengths were dug and barges are said to have travelled between the Greyhound Inn at Coleford and Edford. Remains of the viaduct and a cutting are still to be seen nearby.

Compton Bishop

The village lies in a valley under Crook Peak on the western end of Mendip. It is 600 feet up, although it does not give the impression of being so high. One of the finest views of this attractive small village is from the slopes of Crook Peak itself, the church catching the eye and the roofs pleasingly varied in their angles. Compton Bishop derives from ownership by the Bishop of Bath and Wells, although it was taken into the possession of the crown in the fifteenth century.

So distinctive is the shape of the Peak that it has long been used as a guide for ships out on the tricky waters of the Bristol Channel and was one of the series of great Beacons which warned the rest of the country of the approach of the Armada. Beneath the hill lies a large cave with a magnificent arched roof. Crook Peak and Wavering Down are owned by the National Trust.

The church of St. Andrew dates from the thirteenth century, with some stained glass still in existence from 1375. There is a fine and delicately carved stone pulpit and the treasure includes chalices and a paten from the seventeenth century. Manor Farm House also dates from the seventeenth century and retains its mullioned windows.

Compton Martin

A pretty village set on the lower slopes of north-western Mendip, with an ancient duckpond, though recent works have made it look more like a little reservoir than a traditional pond. An outflow from this supplies the Blagdon lake below. The busy main road runs below the church close to the pond, making stopping hazardous at times. It is a long village which must have been very tranquil before the coming of the motor car.

Entering from the east, there is a fine Georgian house, with glimpses of others, as well as some attractive old cottages, well bedded into their surroundings. The road curves round to show the church spectacularly set against a dark hill.

The church of St. Michael is above the village. The entrance is welcoming as steps lead through wrought-iron gates hung on the next door school house into a crowded graveyard. Over to the far side is a wide almost-empty area, with few graves. The church has a fine square tower and looks its age, although not particularly beautiful from the outside. This is surprising because Pevsner describes it as 'perhaps the best Norman parish church in Somerset' and it is said to be of national importance, but inside is where the real interest lies.

This is a Norman church which has survived because, when the local people began rebuilding it in the Perpendicular style during the fifteenth century, the foundations started to sink, the arch flattened and one of the pillars became tilted. After buttressing and strengthening it, they ceased work but not before adding a twisted piece of carving to one of the pillars, similar to one found in Durham Cathedral, and a fine black oak screen. They left a totally Norman chancel.

East Cranmore

A very small hamlet now consisting principally of a private school at Cranmore Hall. Like its larger cousin, it lies south of the main road in rolling, down-like country, with some fine old oak trees and copses on the tops of the rises. The turning to the hamlet is by a toll house in perfect condition. Opposite the Hall is a tiny, most attractive and unusual old church which, on closer inspection, turns out to be a private house. There is a stubby turret topped by a spire with a window full of house plants inside, and a wooden rose arbour outside.

St. James originally was a Saxon church which was heavily rebuilt in the early nineteenth century. In Victorian times Cranmore Hall was rebuilt from much earlier remains and is a large and impressive building well-suited to a school.

A notable feature of the area is a tower or folly erected 900 feet up on the hillside by J.M. Paget in 1862. There are contradictions about this tower. Some state it has never been opened to the public, others that it was originally open on two days a week.

West Cranmore

The village lies peacefully off the main Shepton Mallet/Frome road where the land flattens, with its church prominent against the open, rolling landscape.

In view of its ancient provenance it is a surprisingly uninspiring village, with its old heart hidden within newer and not particularly attractive buildings. Its fame now lies in the railway and museum founded by David Shepherd, the artist so well known for his superb, detailed pictures of wildlife, steam railway and

landscape. The East Somerset Railway runs short excursions from the halt and is a mecca for many enthusiasts. The original railway operated from 1858 until 1963; it was reopened in 1975 by Prince Bernhard of the Netherlands.

There are nearby quarries supplying a particularly hard stone. Waterlip Quarry used to have a narrow-gauge line feeding the main railway.

The village was known as Crenemelle at the time of Domesday but came back into history when the church of St. Bartholomew was built in the sixteenth century. This has a fifteenth century tower and a Georgian front.

Croscombe

One of the most attractive villages on Mendip, set on the edges of the southern slope, east of Wells. At first sight it seems spoiled by the busy main road running through the centre, but much of the village is above this and, somehow, even the main road area survives untainted. It is remarkable for the quality of its old houses.

Seen from Dinder, Croscombe is very picturesque, with the spire of the church in the distance, the whole fitting perfectly into the curve of the valley. The main road curves through the village, the bulk of the housing to the north, with steep lanes winding up, and everywhere the dark, warm stone of the area. The church is tucked into a fold of the hill, the churchyard packed and constrained by its surroundings. Nearby the Manor House sits opposite a watermill where the River Sheppey roars and creams as it is diverted to increase the flow.

Croscombe has a long history and was far larger in former days when it was one of the primary wool towns of Somerset, nearly half the size of Wells. In the sixteenth and seventeenth centuries there was a population of over 600. The name has changed gradually over the years, from Correges cumb in the eighth century to Corscombe around 1300. Maesbury Camp, far above the village, was a large Belgic British fortification covering nearly six acres

Edward III granted a charter for a weekly market but the main prosperity came in the sixteenth and seventeenth centuries with sheep and wool processing. The wool was washed and cleaned, spun and woven, these activities still being reflected in local names such as Rack Close. There is a fourteenth century Market Cross on the side of the main road. At the end of the nineteenth century local authorities decided to remove it to provide more room for traffic. Unfortunately, they broke the cross and were then attacked by the villagers who saved and mended it, replacing it in its present position.

The Industrial Revolution brought poverty to the area as trade was lost to northern towns with their new machinery. Now it is a quiet residential village once more, with a couple of pubs.

Manor House, Croscombe.

The fifteenth and sixteenth century Church of St. Mary is of great architectural interest as well as being extremely handsome. It represents one of the most remarkable surviving examples of Jacobean carved wood work in the country, while the tower, with its stone spire – the only one in Somerset – is said to be amongst the finest. The oak carvings include an enormous screen, bench ends, three-decker pulpit and roof. Quite apart from this, it is set most attractively among the houses, a perfect village church commanding its population from above.

Dean
This tiny hamlet lies down a cul-de-sac to the north of the Shepton/Frome road and consists of a single street edged with a little cascading stream.

There are a number of enchanting old cottages on one side, while it becomes semi-industrial further up on the other. It is a most delightful, secluded place of peace off one of the busiest roads in the area, with tipper after tipper lorry roaring past on their way to and from the nearby quarries.

Dinder

Another most delightful village on the southern side of Mendip, set between Wells and Shepton Mallet. Here the River Sheppey has been tamed into a series of weirs as it runs beside the old High Street. This leat is said to have been made originally to enable the villagers to dip their buckets in the stream without effort. There is a most attractive row of sixteenth century stone cottages opposite, with fine freestone windows, and a former public house still hangs out its sign of The Dragon on the Wheel.

The village is off the main road to the north, reached through warm stone walls of a similar colour to Draycott stone with its strong pink tinge. Georgian Dinder House, with its unusual front elevation and big windows, is set to the south and partly screened from the road. It was owned by the Somervilles for generations until the fighting Admiral of the Fleet, Sir James Somerville, died there in 1947. Behind the church stands a Queen Anne house with a carved shell over the door said to commemorate the old Glastonbury pilgrims. They used a nearby well to wash their feet on the weary journey from Winchester.

The handsome church of St. Michael is fifteenth century Perpendicular, with some Norman carvings still visible. There are fragments of the original stained glass still in existence, as well as a Norman wall and seventeenth century stone pulpit. A modern memorial commemorates the Admiral who had the unenviable task of destroying the Vichy French fleet at Oran in the Second World War. An ancient yew in the churchyard is believed to be as much as a thousand years old.

Impressive Sharcombe Grange stands high up above the village, commanding a splendid view. Its gates open electrically, for all the world like an American movie.

In Domesday times Dinder was called Denrenn, meaning the 'valley between the woods', a still apposite description for this beautiful spot. One of the finest aspects of it is looking across from the main road to the big house and the church, with the village roofs beyond.

Doulting

A small village outside Shepton Mallet on the Frome road, with a somewhat austere centre which can appear rather dark because of its location in relation to the light. Traffic rushes up the hill from Shepton and round the corner, barely realising there is a village there. But the heart at the cross-roads has very handsome dressed stone buildings – that lovely rectangular square-edged stone so beloved of Georgian builders in the finest of our towns. This famous Doulting stone, used in the construction of a number of famous buildings, is dug from a local quarry.

The curious remote church at Doulting, high above Shepton Mallet.

The church of St. Aldhelm is well worth visiting. With its octagonal tower topped with a spire, it holds court at the entrance to the village at the top of the hill. It is approached up a side road and has the appearance of a cathedral close, with an imposing eighteenth century vicarage lying off to one side. The gates are of elaborate bow-shaped ironwork and a tiny tower contains some slender, ancient windows. In spite of the busy main road, it is remarkably tranquil.

King Ina's nephew, Aldhelm, returned to the village of his formative years to die in the little church that stood here in 709. The King gave Doulting to

Glastonbury in his honour and the monks replaced the wooden chapel with a stone church which was later rebuilt by the Normans. St. Aldhelm's Well is the source of the Sheppey and there is a famous medieval barn nearby.

Downhead

This scattered hamlet lies off the old road from Wells to Frome, in the middle of the plateau. At one stage it supported a local school but now it has a remote, shut-off feel. The cottages are built of a grey stone with warming flecks of yellow, and look most attractive.

The village is widely spread, indeed one might ask if it is a village or a meeting point for scattered farms and their cottages. There are some modern bungalows but most are old, of traditional design.

For many centuries a quarry was the main feature; now there is no sign of it, other than a sheet of water marked on the map. There used to be a narrow-gauge railway serving this quarry from the Waterlip tramway below.

The other distinctive feature is All Saints church and its surrounding houses, which sit alone, stark in the rolling countryside. The church is a most unusual building in three sections, the Perpendicular tower being short and squat, with a high-roofed section dropping down to a newer, lower nave. Eight strange figures with open mouths look down on the world below. Inside, much is modern in concept, but the tower shows its ancient lineage and is worth seeing for the quality and warmth of its stone.

Alongside and behind the church a line of terraced buildings, the largest on the east, the others cottages, sit solidly and delightfully, looking across their gardens over the top of a long stone wall to two large farms.

Draycott

An extensively built-up village on the warm southern slopes of Mendip, popular and attractive in spite of all the infilling. It is notable for the warm red stone quarried locally. This stone is beautiful as exterior building material but also takes a high polish like marble.

It is one of the famous strawberry villages of the area, with a station on the Strawberry Line until its closure in the 1960's. The warm slopes are ideal for market garden crops, and strawberries in particular; nearby growers have stalls on the main road where visitors may take advantage of their quality. Heavy rainfall and long hours of sun have produced early crops for many centuries. It is only the coming of the aeroplane and berries flown in from warmer climes which have cut back their pre-eminence. Every June the village holds its Strawberry Fair, which is deservedly very popular.

The church of St. Peter is Victorian, although it contains a paten from the eighteenth century.

Dulcote

A pleasant, slender village sitting under the southern Mendip slopes, looking across some splendid parkland oaks. The only problem must be the constant traffic on this busy road between Wells and Shepton Mallet. There is a fine old mill house to the north, with rows of neat detached stone cottages on the same side. Perhaps the most interesting part is the sharp bend in the road past a fountain playing up through a huge stone. Closer examination reveals this to be fed by a natural stream.

There are some very attractive houses away from the main road, some in handsome red-tinted sandstone, others with warm and cool mixtures of grey flecked with yellow. Mendip stone varies from village to village all along this road.

Two paper mills operated in Dulcote in the early 1700s. driven by the Sheppey, which played such an important role in this area.

Easton

That part of the village on the main road from Cheddar to Wells has a modern appearance and is passed through in a few moments, but the bulk of the village where the winding lanes reach up into the steep hillsides, is much older . The edge of Mendip is very grand at this point, with woods sloping down into canyons and farmhouses dotting the patchwork of fields. The local stone is grey, but does not give an oppressive feeling.

There is a curious building on the main road which at first glance looks like a non-conformist chapel, but is actually the parish church of St. Paul, built in the mid-nineteenth century. Having become accustomed to the great towers of Somerset, it seems strange and almost out of place to see a church without one.

Ebbor Gorge

This wild spot is set on the southern slopes of Mendip above Wells. Well-wooded, with high cliffs, the way through the magnificent Gorge goes along a steep, stepped footpath, giving a circular route back to the car-park. It is a mile long and the cliffs rise as high as four hundred feet in places, though they are more accessible in most parts. It is owned by the National Trust.

There are caves in the area in which the remains of Stone Age inhabitants were discovered. It is a popular spot with marvellous views over to Glastonbury Tor; well worth a special visit, preferably in sunny weather.

Emborough

This tiny, spread-out hamlet is set on the top of the middle plateau on the road from Wells to the Old Down Inn, with parts hidden in the surrounding country. There is a row of ten or so cottages set together beside the road, probably the extent of the original hamlet, with some gaunt Mendip farmhouses nearby. On the opposite side lies Emborough Pond, looking rather like an artificial reservoir; its dam prevents any flooding of the road a couple of feet below it. Before it was built, this attractive sheet of natural water must have been much larger.

St. Mary's Church, Emborough, overlooking Mendip edge.

Nearby is a farm which used to be the Manor House, said to be the oldest on the Mendip Hills and owned by the Hippisley family from the time of Elizabeth I to the present day, although they lived mainly in nearby Ston.

The most notable building is the church of St. Mary, situated down a lane and looking over Mendip edge. It is most unusual in being painted cream with stone edgings; a squared-off, plain building with a low tower, but a sense of dignity. The church register dates from the mid-1500s and there is a chalice from much the same period. The building is exposed and heavily weathered, with signs of considerable rebuilding in the body. Inside there is a white-washed ceiling and much simply carved stone. It is an unusual and unexpected sight on turning the corner which brings it into view.

Green Ore
Green Ore is a hamlet set round one of the crossroads in the area, where two long straight roads meet on the way from Wells to Bath and Bristol. The Ploughboy Inn has some neighbouring cottages, while on the other side of this busy road is a large modern horticultural establishment specialising in topsoil and turf, in contrast to the sprawling deserted garage opposite.

There is controversy about the meaning of the name. One school believes it was called after the coloured lead ores found in the area, another subscribes to the view that Green Ore is derived from a Saxon word meaning 'farm house'. Since it was a notable centre for lead-mining, practical thoughts lean towards the former view.

The old Grange had connections with the Friary at Witham, in common with the land at nearby Charterhouse. The present house was built in the seventeenth century, replacing an earlier one.

Nearby, there is a monument to Rome in the statue of a she-wolf suckling two human babies, Romulus and Remus. It was erected by a homesick Italian prisoner of war, although he must have grown to like the Mendips because he remained in the area after 1945.

Gurney Slade
A pretty name for a less than beautiful place on Mendip top. This old quarrying village has been heavily built over in recent years and is now quite sizeable. Some years ago it was described as having 'simple stone houses in the old quarrying tradition', but these are now rather lost among rows of uninspiring bungalows and houses.

The village grew in size in support of the quarries for which it supplied labour. In the last century a symbiosis developed which suited both industry and workers alike. In winter they worked for Oakhill Brewery in their busy season, then spent the summer outside in the quarries. Now it has largely lapsed into being a Mendip commuter village.

East Harptree

One of the northern fringe villages set on the slopes above the main road from Churchill to Bristol, where the bleak outlines of western Mendip soften to rolling pastures. East Harptree looks the traditional English village, with old houses of rich red stone set in a maze of roads and lanes, having no obvious centre and little apparent concession to modernity. A peaceful village, pretty and looking as if it had long been embedded in the countryside, it has quite a history behind it.

East Harptree cottages typifying this attractive village.

The sparse remains of Richmont Castle lie below and to the east of the village. This castle supported Queen Matilda against her husband, King Stephen, who arrived in 1138 to besiege it. The owner, Sir William de Harptree, held it successfully until he was deceived into leaving in pursuit of the King's men when they pretended to retreat. When he emerged, cavalry rushed forward to capture the castle. However, it was not knocked down until the reign of King Henry VIII, when its stone was used to build nearby Eastwood House.

In the late 1800s East Harptree joined in the lead exploitation boom and had its own smelting works, reclaiming earlier tailings. Smitham Chimney still stands above the village, one of the very few mining remains.

The Castle of Comfort Inn dates from the mid-eighteenth century while Harptree Court is a long low house built in the early 1800s, with a portico and columns.

The Church of St. Lawrence was originally Norman and retains its doorway, with a thirteenth century chancel. There is a Jacobean pulpit and various treasures from the seventeenth century, but perhaps the most remarkable feature is a monument to Sir John Newton, dating from 1568, with statues of his twenty children kneeling at the base. Amongst the treasures is a Roman pewter vessel found in a nearby field in 1887. It contained coins from the time of nine emperors, mostly dating from the fourth century. Apparently the finders were searching for a spring in a dry period.

West Harptree
Sits below its hillside cousin, on the main road to Weston-super-Mare. An attractive, open village with a centre and defined edges, spoiled only by the traffic rushing through, although this is less of a problem than in some of the narrower village streets elsewhere. Like many Somerset villages, it is deceptive to judge it only by the part visible on the main road, for it spreads widely, particularly towards Chew Valley Lake below. This explains the presence of shops and a bank in such an apparently small place.

Two fine manor houses of great age and splendid condition are near the church. Gournay Court was called after the Norman Gurney family whose names appear elsewhere, as in Gurney Slade. The existing house is seventeenth century, built of the delightful local red-brown sandstone on the site of an earlier mansion. Tilly, or Tilley, Manor House, now an antiques showroom, was built in the mid-1600s and altered again in the eighteenth century, retaining great charm and superb proportions. There is a room over the porch, a stone balcony and fine staircase, together with beautiful gardens which fit the period perfectly.

In the seventeenth century the largest cavern in Somerset was found by lead workers at nearby Lamb Leer. The beehive-shaped cavern is over a hundred feet in each dimension, including height, and has unusual coloured stalactites. There was a paper mill in Harptree in the eighteenth century.

The handsome church of St. Mary sits at the heart, occupying a corner between two roads and suiting the character of the village perfectly. A Norman tower has had a graceful spire added, but much of the rest of the church was rebuilt by the Victorians. There is an interesting remnant of a porch with space over it for the choir.

Holcombe

A most interesting village on the north-western side of the plateau because it dates from after the Black Death. This plague reduced the population of the original village to one person and a decision was taken to build anew a couple of miles away on a windblown hill top. Now all that remains of the original village is the church, although the new village even built its own church to be conveniently near at hand.

The present village is not particularly attractive, consisting principally of a long street with a mixture of houses spread over a considerable distance, with shops and a post office dropped in at random. A large transport company feeds the quarry and the place has clearly grown considerably in recent years. At the top of the hill there is a manor house and one or two substantial older buildings at what must have been the original and attractive heart of the village.

However, the church from the old village still exists. Holcombe Old Church of St. Andrew is more than worth the effort of searching for it. A lane goes by a farmyard and through an open gate to curve round a large field until the church comes into view, framed in trees at the bottom of the valley. It is a delightful scene: the ancient church is beautifully looked-after in a well-tended churchyard. It is such a peaceful spot, one of Mendip's unexpected treasures.

Inside, the church retains Georgian box pews and a Jacobean pulpit, light and airy with its white painted woodwork. There is even a reputed Saxon window, as well as some Norman parts. The church has no electricity supply, still using candles.

The parents of Scott of the Antarctic lived in the manor and are buried in the churchyard, with a simple memorial to their famous son on the headstone.

East Horrington

One of two neighbouring villages set five hundred feet above Wells on the upland road to Frome, East Horrington is the last village before Chantry. A small hamlet which has grown in recent years, it has some attractive old cottages amongst more modern building.

The early nineteenth century church of St. John the Evangelist has been closed for a number of years but is a landmark on the road, framing Glastonbury Tor as the traveller descends from Mendip towards Wells.

West Horrington

It is larger than its sister hamlet, but with no church of its own. The village is unusual in that it lies in a cul-de-sac off the main road from Wells to Bath.

The road runs between high stone walls and two large farmyards before winding steeply uphill. There is considerable variation, with irregularly placed houses producing an interesting layout; new and old blend together well, with sweeping views over to Wells and its surrounds. On one steep side the buildings look down on their neighbours opposite. Lanes wander off to the side, making the village larger than expected, tucked under the sheltering hill.

Leigh-on-Mendip

Its prominent church tower catches the eye as the road drops down from the south to show the village spread out below. There is a long, narrow village street, with the ancient heart clustered beside the church, old cottages with low ceilings contrasting with the height of the tower. The village peters out to the west, with a small group of houses or tiny hamlet, before finally edging off into the countryside. There is a quiet air of prosperity and the sense of being a pleasant place in which to live.

The village owes its presence to agriculture and quarrying; the latter still takes place to the east, a great scar in the countryside, clearly visible but not really taking away from the prospect.

Leigh has an ancient history, as is shown by the vicarage and a local farm built in Elizabethan times, while mining continued on over many centuries. On either side of the church are pilgrims' cottages, resting places on the long trip to Glastonbury from Winchester and the east, for this was a well-known route.

It is reported that in the mid-1800s the vicar was shot in the pulpit by a villager whom he had accused of drunkenness. Fortunately, the man was a bad shot, causing only slight damage. At that same period the village had another of the famous ironworks of Fussell's of Mells, of which two chimneys still remain.

St. Giles Church has a magnificent tower, over ninety feet high and built in the fifteenth century. This great building crowds over the churchyard, heavily decorated on the exterior and with a view from the top, it is said, extending as far as Westbury White Horse on a fine day. The benches are very old, with simple carvings on the ends, while the magnificent roof has figures above the beams, looking down on the worshippers in the light and airy nave. It is one of the most inspiring interiors we have come across, imbued with a remarkable sense of quiet and peace.

Leighton

This hamlet lies beyond the great Tor Works of Foster Yeoman, with its Union Jack, beautifully manicured lawns and stark quarry. This enormous gash in the countryside, feeding limestone into the rail network and across the Channel, is remarkably neat and tidy and employs a great many local people.

Leighton is a pretty little hamlet consisting of a farm and farm cottages, with a small chapel of its own. It is hardly noticeable when travelling along the main road, but is very characteristic of old Somerset.

Litton

A most attractive old stone village of remarkably consistent quality, set in a valley with a stream. It is tightly built in on itself because of the constraints forced by the shape of the valley. The heart is a deep narrow road with handsome, substantial old houses and some cottages tucked away on different levels. The stone is a warm grey which melds in with the surrounds, a building material which looks as though it is there to last, not to impress.

The hidden church of St. Mary, Litton.

A stream rushes past the pub, the King's Arms, set off in a courtyard and looking every inch of its fifteenth century origins. The village of Litton is enchanting; high walls make tunnels of the lanes, cottages set down by the edge of the stream, bigger houses up above, all result in a harmonious whole.

Litton Manor was sold to Bishop Giso by King Alfred the Great and was mentioned in Domesday as *Litune*. The area is known to have been extensively farmed before the fourteenth century, while there was a paper mill in the eighteenth century, a relic of a number of mills by the stream in medieval times. Nowadays the village is much smaller and has lapsed into its early 'sleepier' existence.

The church of St. Mary is hidden from the casual eye, set above the village, hidden, a remarkable and ancient house which forms one boundary, its tiny stone windows peering into the churchyard. The church is small and beautiful, with a fourteenth century square tower ornamented with gargoyles, and a nicely proportioned main body. There is a Norman font and stone pulpit from the Perpendicular period. But above all it is an intimate village church of great charm.

Mells

One of the renowned Somerset beauty spots. A larger village of winding lanes, old stone cottages, thatch and a well-balanced layout, it is a strange mixture of rural beauty with a noteworthy industrial past. One of its principal claims to fame is being the home of 'Little Jack Horner' of the old nursery rhyme. He worked for Thomas Cromwell and somehow acquired the village of Mells from Glastonbury Abbey, building himself a splendid manor house there. The 'plum' of the rhyme was the deeds to the village.

Charles I stayed at the Manor House in 1644 in the absence of the then Horner, who was a staunch Parliamentarian. The village stayed in the Horner family from the time of Henry VIII until the early part of this century, when it passed to the political family of Asquith.

The name of the village is taken from the Latin, *mellis*, meaning honey, as recorded when it became part of Glastonbury Abbey's possessions in the tenth century. Later, Abbot Selwood of Glastonbury rebuilt some of the village to a modern layout.

The mid-eighteenth century found wool prosperity gripping the village, and John Wesley preached there in 1785. At one stage there was a coal pit in Mells but it reached the peak of its industrial fame with the ironfounders, Fussell's of Mells, who made a variety of tools in the nineteenth century, achieving countrywide fame for their quality. Mells River provided the power and the coal the heat for the forges. The remains of the works may be found nearby, though long closed.

The fifteenth century church of St. Andrew sits alongside the manor house, forming a group said by Pevsner to be 'among the happiest in Somerset'. This magnificent church has a tower and spire of over one hundred feet in height, of particularly handsome appearance. Some of the benches are Jacobean, while there are some fine modern bench ends carved by local craftsmen, as well as some stained glass from the fifteenth century. Inside, there is an equestrian monument by Sir Alfred Munnings and a peacock carved by Burne-Jones.

A corner of handsome Mells.

Nettlebridge

Driving north from Shepton Mallet to Bath, a curve reveals this hamlet lying below the road on its built-up viaduct, except for the Nettlebridge Inn and one or two houses which are actually on the road. It is all too easy to drive quickly through without realising the history behind this scatter of buildings.

The quiet peace belies the closed-down coal mines of the last century and the bustle and pace of constructing a canal which was never to open. The last remains of this unfortunate venture may still be found nearby.

Nunney

There is a delightful view of the village from the main Frome/Shepton road, with colour-washed houses ranged along the upper slopes, before dropping down to the ancient cottages in the centre, some of which date back to the seventeenth century. At the very heart lies the castle, with a brook flowing between it and the high street. Nunney is one of those rare places which does not disappoint the visitor; church, castle and surrounding stone houses provide a feast for the eye.

The village is said to have been founded by a Saxon called *Nunna*, well over a thousand years ago. A form of his name is found in the Domesday Book, where the village was called *Nouin*.

In 1645 a Parliamentary force attacked the fourteenth century castle. The first shots smashed holes in the apparently massive, but actually flimsy, walls and the garrison surrendered immediately – not one of the most glorious incidents of the period. The road into Nunney never fails to surprise, with an unexpected view of the castle rising like a medieval mirage. A moat surrounds the rectangular walls, from inside which the church stands framed through a stone window. A bridge crosses the stream, leading to the main street with its unusual inn sign bridging the road. Nearby there is a recently restored ancient Guard House, where people were held under charges in the past.

In the early 1800s there was a factory making superior hand-made cloth, together with the ubiquitous, if small, Fussell's of Mells works.

Nowadays a Street Fair takes place on the first Saturday in August, revived from ancient custom after the Queen's Silver Jubilee.

The thirteenth century church of All Saints was built by the de la Mare family, but restored in the nineteenth century. A Norman font remains, together with a number of early de la Mare tombs. There is a remarkable wall painting depicting St. George, which is believed to date from the fourteenth century.

Oakhill

A strange mixture, with little to recommend much of it aesthetically, but some interesting buildings, particularly along the main road. Among these is an elaborate nineteenth century Congregational church, made into two houses some years ago and, dating from 1825, an elegant Methodist church with handsome pointed windows, set among older stone buildings. Trav elling towards Bath, past Oakhill House with it ornate gates, the village stretches for a considerable distance with a number of large, solid stone buildings of understated elegance. The road then winds its way down the valley.

Oakhill was barely a hamlet until the mid-1700s, when the great John Billingsley founded the Brewery and built nearby Ashwick Court, from where he conducted many of the affairs of the county and discoursed on the agriculture of the time. The brewing tradition is carried on to this day, although not on the scale of the nationally sold Oakhill Stout of the nine-teenth century. At that time, the majority of houses were brewery-owned, let to its workers. The brewery had pubs all over Somerset and Wiltshire, as well as in Bristol, and by the early part of this century the famous Oakhill Stout was available over much of England, moved by rail. A narrow-gauge private line linked up with the main line at Binegar, but in 1925 a disastrous fire destroyed the brewery, forcing a shut down. By that time the firm owned over 170 pubs which they continued to run, but eventually the name van-ished when these were taken over.

The Church of All Saints was built in the mid-nineteenth century, at much the same time as a Church of England School, well after the Methodist Chapel.

Priddy

A remote place of high rainfall but with an inbuilt charm all its own and a long and fascinating history; at eight hundred feet Priddy is the highest village in Somerset, and said to be the oldest agricultural village on Men-dip. A thatched stack of hurdles on a wide green denotes the village's most famous event, the annual Sheep Fair, which has been held each August for over six hundred years, ever since Priddy took over the Fair from Wells. In 1348, at the time of the Black Death. In the early days of this century it was the most notable day on Mendip with gypsies, horse copers, prize fighting and other delights, as well as the main business of buying and selling ani-mals. 1994 was the 647th year, still on the same site and still run by a com-mittee of local shareholders.

The village abounds with early history, being remarkable for the rich-ness and abundance of the prehistoric remains surrounding it. Among the most notable are Bronze Age Priddy Nine Barrows near the Miners Arms and Eight Barrows on Ashen Hill. Further over near the Castle of Comfort are the Priddy Circles, four mysterious Bronze Age earth rings, each over five-hundred feet across, standing in a row and over a mile long, with a

Roman road nearby. Tumuli and camps combine to make this one of the most interesting and important sites of the area.

Priddy has always been a centre of mining on Mendip. There are traces of workings before the Romans, who continued the tradition. Lead was mined until the end of the seventeenth century and again in the nineteenth, when new processes enabled the extraction of further metal from the old tailings. Nearby Priddy Pool lies in a turbulent sea of gruffy ground, looking like a giant's battle field. The old horizontal flues are still visible. Priddy is one of the four mineries, which were the property of the Lords Royal of Mendip, where miners brought ore to be washed before final reduction to metal in the furnaces.

In the mid-nineteenth century a piped trough was installed in the village to give the first pure water supply. Now there is a borehole and pumped reservoir for the village. Prior to that a few dew ponds, together with Priddy Pool, gave the only open areas of water on Mendip. Carts, then lorries, hauled water for cattle and sheep elsewhere. Even now with modern tarmac roads, it is possible to realise how hard life must have been up on these harsh hills before modern communications took over.

The area is also famous for its caves, of which Swildon's Hole has been described as the 'most magnificent cave in Britain and one with some of the most beautiful underground scenery.' The village is the unofficial headquarters of the cavers, who are usually to be seen loading or unloading nearby, or gathering to tell their tales in the pubs.

The parish church of St. Lawrence stands high up overlooking the green, washed by rain and often bathed in cloud. It was built in the thirteenth century but rebuilt in the fifteenth in a Gothic style. It has a Perpendicular stone altar, Norman font and Tudor oak screen. A five-hundred year old altar cloth with flowers embroidered in gold thread remains under glass in perfect condition, bringing home the continuity of life in rural Britain.

A local legend suggests that Joseph of Arimathea visited Priddy in his capacity as a lead merchant. Glastonbury, visible with much of the Levels from a nearby scarp, also claims a visit from Joseph, who is said to have founded the first church there.

Rodney Stoke

One of the villages on the Wells/Axbridge road, famous for strawberry-growing on the warm southern slopes of Mendip, set among rolling hills. The lovely old buildings are of the local red Dolomitic sandstone, quarried nearby since Roman times until this century. It is known as Draycott Marble when polished and has been used to produce some remarkable tables and other pieces.

Originally, King John presented the village to a Baron called Stoke Giffard but the name was changed to celebrate the marriage of a member of the family to a Rodney. One of their descendants was the great admiral who was such a scourge of Napoleon's navy. Now all that remains of the original Rodney mansion is a gatehouse close to the church.

The twelfth century church of St. Leonard's was rebuilt during the fifteenth century. It contains a number of tombs of the Rodney family, the oldest dating from 1478, with a memorial to the famous admiral. The twelfth century stone font has a Jacobean cover and the tower is notable for bells going back to before 1500.

Rowberrow

It is difficult to imagine that Rowberrow Bottom contained a village as big as Shipham in the eighteenth century. Now it is a straggly little hamlet, almost joined to its larger neighbour. At the centre is the Swan, with the other cottages and farms dotted around. The only real indication of a village is the sign on one lane – School Road. The Parish Church lies half a mile away, tucked into a corner on a steep bank. Behind it are glimpses of a large, yellow-painted house. The Old Rectory is nearby, with beech hedges surmounting eight-feet stone walls. It has wicket gates set in the wall and is the very stuff of Victorian/Gothic novels.

Today Rowberrrow is well known for the Swan Inn, which draws in customers from miles around. In spite of looking like a cottage, albeit with extensions added, the interior bars are very roomy.

Rowberrow Camp is believed to have been of Roman origin, as is the track which runs into and beyond it, while an earlier tumulus lies near the church. Its known history goes back to medieval times, and in the eighteenth century it is mentioned as a centre for mining calamine. However, by the end of that century demand ceased, throwing over one thousand miners out of work and causing dreadful poverty. The trade must have come back later because it was noted how the fumes from its burning were poisoning the vegetation in the area.

The church of St. Michael is a strange mixture of ancient and Victorian restoration. Its fifteenth century tower, with an outside bulge denoting an interior staircase, is in warm red sandstone. The whole church is small, having some Victorian 'improvement', with the exception of an unusually high chimney. There is a small churchyard on two sides only, packed with graves on every slope, many of them very old.

Shipham

The square is the heart of Shipham, with a garage, shops and the Miners Arms on two sides. The Penscot Farmhouse Hotel is distinctive, long and low behind a wide grassy space. Unfortunately, this attractive area is rather spoilt by a mass of overhead cables. A pole in the middle of the green has wires radiating out from it. The outlying lanes are worth searching out; the stone walls and cottages give Shipham its unusual character, many being built rapidly and haphazardly to accommodate miners during the calamine 'boom' of the eighteenth century. And everywhere there are glimpses of bracken and hills, with stunning views beyond to the Bristol Channel. However, these can be obscured by the mists that abound at this height.

Outside the village on the upper slopes, there is an impression of Devon lanes, with hedges on high banks and a mass of wild flowers in season. On the way to Cheddar, many people stop at Lilypool Cider and Cheese Farm for a local souvenir or bottle of cider.

Shipham has always been a mining centre and minerals can still cause problems. In 1979 the villagers were told to stop eating their own produce because of a scare over cadmium poisoning, although this was cleared and has now passed into history. Old mine refuse has long made the ground difficult to cultivate, reducing output.

Calamine was mined from the sixteenth to eighteenth century and beyond. The main supplies of the ore were sent to the Bristol brass works but, in common with Rowberrow, the ups and downs of the industry had devastating effects on the people, causing severe poverty at times. This brought with it lawlessness; indeed it was said that towards the end of the eighteenth century no constable dare go up to arrest a Shipham man. At this time Hannah More started one of her schools in an effort to provide training, reduce drunkenness and help the children.

The village of *Sipeham* was mentioned in Domesday, the name coming from the Saxon, meaning hamlet of sheep – appropriate still. At one corner of the square, the church of St. Leonard is on such a steep slope that passersby on the road above look down on the tower. It was built in the mid-nineteenth century and restored again some ninety years ago, but a register goes back to the sixteenth century and an earlier building.

Stoke St. Michael

Set in attractive countryside, the road goes past Wainwright's quarries with their piles of grit and stones, screened by out-of-place conifers. With a mixture of old and new houses, the outskirts are rather grey and uninteresting before opening up into a much more attractive heart huddled across and alongside a stream. The village is far larger than might at first be imagined and the centre reflects this, with shops and the seventeenth century Knatchbull Arms. The church is nearby, as well as the remains of an Elizabethan manor which once belonged to the Dukes of Buckingham. Next to the pub there is another remarkable small manor house, of some age.

To confuse matters, the village has been known as Stoke Lane and the nearby hamlet of Stoke Bottom had a number of mills powered by the river. This stream has caused problems to the village, flooding so badly at times that holes had to be knocked in garden walls to clear the waters. In the 1920s there was a flourishing creamery, but this has long vanished with rationalisation.

The church of St. Michael is a most unusual looking building, made even more so by the bright pink main door. It was rebuilt in the nineteenth century but fortunately some older parts were preserved.

Stratton on the Fosse

Famous as the home of the school, monastery and great abbey of Downside, as well as a village in its own right.

Dominating the skyline, the Abbey is visible from far off. Curiously, some distinctive hills beyond seem higher, even though the building appears to be on the top of the world. Manicured grass fields, with hedges neatly trimmed, lead up to the village. Stratton is an unexpectedly attractive place – an old village, very much on different levels, with warm grey stone, similar to the old parts of Frome.

The huge Abbey is bigger than some cathedrals, being part of a much larger complex started after the Benedictine monks were forced out of France during the French Revolution. They bought the mansion of Mount Pleasant just after Waterloo and have added to it ever since. The culmination came this century with the building of the great Abbey, with its 166 feet tower and enormous vaulted nave in the Gothic tradition, which is a memorial to those killed in the Great War. One of the architects was the great Sir Gilbert Scott. It is now part of a Catholic public school, with more than five hundred pupils taught by the monks. The school buildings stretch in a wide front across the Abbey.

The Roman Fosse Way running through the village has ensured its continuing importance through the centuries. Stratton belonged to Glastonbury Abbey until William the Conqueror gave it to one of his Bishops, who rebuilt the church, which is one of only two in Britain dedicated to St. Vigor. In time the manor passed to the ubiquitous Gurneys, who seemed to claim ownership of so much of this area in the thirteenth century, although eventually it became a part of the Duchy of Cornwall. Stratton lies on the Somerset coalfield which formerly produced much coal. The start of the Dorset & Somerset Canal was to have been at this point, running through to Frome to take the coal to its markets elsewhere.

The original small church of St. Vigor sits above the road, surrounded by lovely old houses. Much rebuilding took place in the eighteenth century but it retains its charm, together with some of the old features, including a fifteenth century stone Perpendicular pulpit and stained glass. An unusual feature is the organ, originally made for Brighton Pavilion.

Vobster

A village divided into two parts, quite separate, but looking up and down at each other, and very different in character. From Leigh-on-Mendip the road crosses a stream, one of the forks of the Vallis, before entering the lower part of the village by the Vobster Inn, which looks as though it has been made up from a row of small cottages. Nearby the Old Post Office, a delightful cream cottage with black windows and ledges, is rounded, comfortable and plastered, part of this little group of houses which looks quite unlike others in the area.

Upper Vobster is along a No Through Road above, looking down on the church. This area has a mixture of old and new, but with a great sense of space and height. It is surprising to think of this as a coal mining and quarrying village because any signs are well hidden. The name alone makes it worth a visit.

The church of St. Edmund was built in the mid-nineteenth century and looks as if it should have had a tower. It is set in a field between the two parts of the village and access looks difficult, being along narrow country roads with no footpath.

Waterlip

A little hamlet above Cranmore which formerly consisted only of a line of seventeenth century almshouses. Now there is some industry and it is well scattered, with a transport company and an engineering concern, together with other rather derelict-looking sites. The remains of a quarry lie to one side and there are a couple of large farms.

Waterlip limestone quarry was known for its horse-drawn narrow gauge tramway built in 1870. Later this was converted to steam, and finally to standard gauge in the 1920s. In its heyday it carried over 20,000 tons of limestone each year down to Cranmore station and the main line. The line was extended to two other quarries before finally shutting.

Westbury-sub-Mendip

Another one of the strawberry villages on the road from Axbridge to Wells, this village is far larger than perceived from the road. Several lanes wander up into the hill or down to the moor. There are a number of timeless substantial stone houses.

On the southern slope of the main road there is a most unusual angled row of modern houses. It is good to see a farmyard right in the middle. Stone walls, an ancient cross and a triangle complete the picture. The church is down a cul-de-sac to the south, beside a manor house. The neighbouring building looks as if it might have been a turnpike cottage.

The surrounding countryside has high walls with farms and buildings set back under the greenest of hills, with extensive views of rolling countryside to the south. Many rhinoceros and other bones have been found at nearby Westbury Quarry. The village was recorded in Domesday as *Westberie* and still celebrates the existence of a Friendly Society started in the eighteenth century.

The Church of St. Lawrence is a gem, set near huge trees in a peaceful churchyard away from the noise of the main road. It is of varying ages, however, with a chancel dating from the thirteenth century and a tower which is still supported by a Norman arch inside although much was re-built in the late nineteenth century. The remains of a blocked up Norman doorway are visible on the outside. The great yew tree in the churchyard is said to be over eight hundred years old.

Whatley

Together with nearby Chantry, is at the eastern gateway to Mendip, set on the plateau just before the hill road from Wells and Shepton Mallet drops down to Frome.

The village is widely spread, with farms and cottages scattered over some distance, much of it extremely pretty. There are some lovely old stone houses and a splendid manor house. The countryside is steep, with woods and plough-ground, and banks of snowdrops along the road in the spring.

The only problem in these narrow country roads is the number of stone-carrying lorries. This is quarry country and the upper end of the village is grey with stone-dust from nearby Whatley Combe quarry.

Whatley has been in existence at least since Roman times; there are remains of both paving and a bath nearby. In common with many parts round here, the manor was granted to Glastonbury Abbey. In the nineteenth century a rector of Whatley became Dean of St. Paul's and was later buried in the village. Some industry existed then, with the production of high quality cloth and a small Fussell's of Mells factory. Now the village has gone back to its previous rural quiet.

The church of St. George has some remnants of its thirteenth century origin but was heavily restored twice in the last century. There is a tower with a pleasing octagonal spire, which is widely visible. The well-kept building stands in a large, rather bare churchyard flanked by a farmyard, very much in the rural tradition.

Wookey Hole

Set in the southern slopes of Mendip to the west of Wells, Wookey Hole is famous for its great cave system and a traditional, working, hand-made paper mill. It is a charming village, once past the nearby EMI works set in what looks like a prisoner-of-war camp. Is this really the face of our high-tech defence industry? The remainder is largely the result of a model village built by the owners of the paper mill a century ago. There is a Gothic church, together with a small Gothic school where H.G. Wells once taught.

However, for visitors to Wookey Hole, the centre must be the complex which houses a show-ground museum, the paper mill and the entrance to the famous caves, now owned by Madame Tussaud. The name Wookey is said to arise from the Celtic name for a cave. The River Axe, which emerges at this point, gave birth to the paper-mills which have existed at least since the seventeenth century.

The caves are still being explored, with caverns discovered by intrepid divers making their way through sumps to reach one from another. Documents surviving from the fifteenth century mention both the caves and the legend of a woman living in them who was believed to have caused all sorts of local mayhem. A monk from Glastonbury sprinkled holy water on her, turning her to stone; thus, the Witch of Wookey is immortalised in the form of a stalagmite in the main cave. The tale was given substance in 1912 when a woman's skeleton was found in the floor, with a knife lying nearby.

The first record of man's presence is over 15,000 years ago. Wookey Hole was inhabited during the Iron Age, and Hyena Cave was occupied by Stone Age hunters at a time when rhinoceros, mammoths and other tropical beasts lived on Mendip. Hyena teeth and other bones are on show in the museum. The Romans were known to be in possession of the caves during their occupation of Britain. The last major disturbance to life in Wookey Hole came with the heavy pollution of the waters emerging from the cave, leading to the closure of the lead-smelting works at Priddy.

5 Wildlife & Conservation

Mendip Specialities

Mendip has three special features which make it 'different', worth preserving and of a unique nature. Most obvious are the geology and structure, the caves and relics of prehistoric times. Another feature is the limestone grassland, typical of west Mendip, with its special mixture of wild flowers on sheep-grazed sward; although one of the problems which has to be faced is that some of this is under-grazed, with the subsequent growth of scrub changing the whole character and wildlife. The third feature is the unusual limestone ash woodlands on the north and south faces. These maintain their presence because of the economic problems of changing their nature. All these areas require positive help in their long-term maintenance.

As may be imagined after considering this varied and fascinating landscape of Mendip, there is an equally varied fauna and flora, some of which needs attention if it is to survive. But the innate beauty of the place depends on its basic structure, its natural clothing and the way in which that is cultivated.

This structure, so close to the surface in Mendip with its limestone and sandstone skeleton, should not alter, but the quarrying factor has to be considered. The rate of extraction is so high that parts of the hills are being eaten away at an alarming rate, changing the very shape of the massif and having other hidden effects. Another connected factor is the water-table, which is very much a part of the conservation debate. No-one knows what the effect of a much-altered water table will be, except that it will certainly have repercussions on the Levels since they receive much of their water from under Mendip. Will it also affect surface vegetation on the hills themselves?

Agriculture and Woodlands

In present-day terms, the natural clothing is the permanent grassland and woodland cover, constantly at risk from changes in economic strategy by government and EC, and pressures exerted on incomes of farmers who have to probe the boundaries of farming techniques if they are to survive. Fortunately, some of these pressures are being relieved by changes in attitudes to farm surpluses within the Community. Set-aside may make farms less likely to convert grassland to grain, while the ability of English Nature to declare a site an SSSI – where justified – gives hope for the more important parts at risk.

Woodland is another question where the referees are out at present. Whether Mendip woods survive, increase in area or decrease, depends in part on government policy, which is far from settled at this time. From the conservation point of view there is only one certain solution – for a conservation body to own the woods, although even then a shortage of money may preclude proper use being made of the resources.

The way in which the soil is cultivated is the most important factor of all and depends on markets, grants and subsidies, the balance between each being largely determined by government/EC policies. To conserve flowers and insects sitting at the base of the food-chain, there must be little or no change. Grassland flowers and creatures are best served by the retention of unfertilised and spray-free surrounds, the ancient sward of the old-style farmers, who stock the land lightly, farming at minimum cost – as opposed to maximum yields.

One of the biggest problems for the delicate upland limestone pastures is the pig-breeding industry. Areas at the top of Cheddar Gorge and above Draycott have been given over to outdoor pig-rearing and the native pasture is being damaged and altered permanently. The shallow soil, good drainage and general nature of the area are well-suited to this activity, on marginal land not affected by SSSI status but nevertheless containing quality limestone herbage. However, it is to be hoped that the notorious cycle of pig prices may stop the activity spreading elsewhere.

Woods either need no management at all, relying on the death and decay of old trees to provide natural clearings in which seedlings will regenerate, or a continuation of the system of coppicing, which gives a succession of open glades and heavier shade, suiting many specialist flowers and insects. Unfortunately, much of the woodland is at present in an interim stage, moving from the old coppicing to a state of neglect, but that is better than seeing it vanish beneath the axe.

Sites of Special Scientific Interest (SSSIs)

While part of Mendip is an Area of Outstanding Natural Beauty (AONB), it has not been given the status of an Environmentally Sensitive Area (ESA) by government and it looks as though this is unlikely to happen, given present policies. So what protection can be offered is either in the hands of its owners – farmers or institutions – or through individual arrangements made by English Nature, where parts have been designated Sites of Special Scientific Interest (SSSI).

Where an area is an SSSI farmers may be required to forego certain operations, or change their way of farming so as not to endanger the nature of the site. Where English Nature requires this, compensation is worked out based on the extra costs involved; thus farmers do not suffer from the arrangement in financial terms. All SSSI site-holders are also required to notify English Nature of any changes they may be thinking of making to their farming methods. Negotiations may then take place to compensate for potential loss of income if they are asked not to make these changes. This in itself can lead to abuse but often farmers welcome the chance to keep, or return to, low intensity farming methods without suffering income loss, retaining the traditional methods developed over the ages to suit this countryside.

SSSIs are an extremely valuable method of preserving important natural sites, although they are not always invulnerable to outside destruction or change; sometimes even through government intervention, as in the case of certain roads being pushed through regardless.

Currently, there are twenty-six SSSIs on our part of Mendip, taking up 4,469 acres of land. In broad terms, ten sites are declared principally for geology or palaeontology, fourteen for mainly botanical reasons, one for botany and geology, and one for bats. Many of the botanical sites are notable also for invertebrates – insects, spiders, snails etc. Flora starts the chain of life, with insects following, leading eventually to mammals, so there is logic in the way these SSSIs are determined. Limestone-based Mendip has long been famous for its flora, with ever more being found out about its invertebrate and other wildlife as new surveys are carried out.

Flora and Fauna

The rare flowers for which Mendip is noted include Cheddar Pink, found clinging to the cliffs on inaccessible ledges, Cheddar Bedstraw and Little Robin. Scarce species include Rock Stonecrop, Dwarf Mouse-ear, Purple Gromwell, Pale St. John's-wort, Sea Storksbill, Spring Sandwort, Spring Cinquefoil, Narrow-leaved Bittercress, Narrow-lipped Helleborine, Hornwort and Slender Tare.

But mention should also be made of commoner species, the great sheets of Bluebells to be found in the woods in spring, Wood Anemones by the roadside and in copses, Common Rock-rose and Thyme spreading round the outcrops of limestone and the purple flowers of Meadow Cranesbill everywhere in mid-summer.

Mendip is one of the places where there are some 'real' meadows remaining, with tapestries of flowers of every size and shape mixed and twined into a great carpet of colour. Sheets of Dogs Mercury and Ramsons are to be seen in the woods early on, the breath of garlic drifting up on the breeze. Other places bring Wild Daffodils, while the area is famous for the number and variety of its orchids. The acid soils still sport heathers, though these have diminished over the years. 'Gruffy' ground, such as at Priddy Mineries, is often covered in great tufts of coarse Purple Moor-grass, making walking difficult and uncomfortable, while bracken is found in other areas. But the close-cropped sheep-sward of the limestone area is studded with flowers and is a joy to walk across. Mendip is such a magnificently varied landscape as to make exploration a rewarding process.

The tree population varies considerably, depending on depth of soil, acidity or alkalinity. Some of the varieties which may be found include Small-leaved Lime, Whitebeam, Pedunculate Oak, Ash, Field Maple, Wild Service tree, Wych-elm, Beech and some fine Yews. The under-storey, equally important for variety and colour, has such shrubs or small trees as Hazel, Buckthorn, Wayfaring-tree, Guelder-rose, Crab Apple, Dogwood, Wild Privet and Spindle.

Specialists in fungi report many varieties of these on Mendip and an autumn walk through the older woods is to be recommended. Underfoot and on trees and rocks there are several species of rare, and many common, lichens, as well as numerous mosses and liverworts.

The insect life of Mendip is both abundant and fascinating, although less is known about much of it than the flora. There are so many thousands of species that it is impossible to see even a small proportion. Nevertheless, the area is known for the variety and numbers of many families. For instance, over thirty species of butterflies have been recorded as breeding on Draycott Sleights reserve.

Interesting species of Mendip butterfly include Small Pearl-bordered, High Brown, Silver-washed and Dark Green Fritillaries; White-letter and Purple Hairstreaks; Green Hairstreak – seen in numbers in spring in some parts; Marbled White; Chalkhill, Adonis, Small and Silver-studded Blues; Grizzled and Dingy Skippers; and Grayling.

Mendip is known also for some unusual grasshoppers and crickets, including the Striped-winged Grasshopper and Great Green Bush Cricket, while the ponds at Priddy are especially worth visiting for dragonflies. At times the Water Horsetails are alive with thousands of damselflies and darters emerging simultaneously. Sixteen species breed on these isolated sheets of water, including Emerald Damselfly, Black Darter and Downy Emerald, while twenty species have been seen. The limestone suits a variety of ants, including the rare *Myrmica Schencki*. The Glow-worm is found in some localities, the female attracting the male beetle by the luminous segments on her body.

Emerging darters on Waldegrave Pool.

Bird life is plentiful without being spectacular; rarities are not such regular occurrences as on wetlands. Nevertheless, the woods are full of warblers and other small birds, woodpeckers and birds of prey. Buzzards are more numerous than ever, while Sparrowhawks may be seen hunting the woods and hedgerows regularly, with the occasional sighting of the much larger Goshawk. It is possible to hear the reeling sound of the Grasshopper Warbler in selected parts, the very spirit of summer and warm weather.

That powerful hunter, the Peregrine Falcon, is often seen high over Cheddar Gorge now that its numbers have increased in recent years. Its swoop is one of the great sights of this world, the bird hurtling down on its prey at speeds of well over one hundred miles per hour and rarely missing, leaving a puff of feathers hanging in the air.

Of the area's mammals, the Dormouse is the most interesting, found breeding in many of the woods clustered round Cheddar. Efforts are being made to find out why they should survive here and not in other apparently equally suitable sites. Captive breeding, then letting the young out in the wild in carefully controlled conditions, has had success in colonising nearby woods, and it is hoped they will continue to flourish and increase in number around Cheddar. The cave systems of Mendip support good bat populations, including both Greater and Lesser Horseshoe species.

Badgers are found all over the woods and the Somerset Wildlife Trust organises parties to watch the young at play in selected places, which is particularly popular with children. Lastly, but just as exciting for both young and old, are the deer of Mendip. Roe deer are extremely common, having increased in numbers considerably in recent years. They have changed their habits, from solitary animals only seen at dawn and dusk, to being visible at many times of the day, often in small groups. Not long ago seven were seen walking up the road through Cheddar Gorge. Fallow deer are often present, though much warier, and it is believed that the tiny, pig-like Muntjac is moving into the area.

Conservation Bodies

A number of conservation bodies, either private, semi-governmental or institutional, make important contributions to preserving Mendip. The Wildlife Trusts have been buying up reserves fast in recent years and spend considerable effort and expertise in organizing volunteers to conduct carefully thought-out, long-term, conservation plans, based on methodical surveys of the sites. Their efforts are well worth supporting through membership, where everyone is welcome. The many excellent reserves offer a life-time of opportunities for watching wildlife or just walking in beautiful country-side.

English Nature is the body responsible for advising the government on nature conservation in England. It selects and manages National Nature Reserves and identifies and arranges the management of SSSIs.

It sees Mendip as having great importance for its diversity and for a number of key features. These include herb-rich limestone grasslands, traditional hay meadows; old coppiced woodlands, both for themselves and because they have populations of the Dormouse; caves and mines supporting breeding and roosting sites for bats; the wide-ranging species of invertebrates; and the many geological features, such as gorges, caves and fossil deposits.

The agency looks to restore and enhance grassland communities; encourage traditional woodland management; ensure protection of rare bat species; and influence land use, with particular emphasis on quarrying, to ensure that wildlife and geological features are not damaged.

Present worries include lack of sufficient finance to support proper grassland management; lack of suitable markets for coppice products; the destruction of regenerating woodland by the present large deer population; ever-increasing demands for quarried limestone. Some current advantages are the positive interest taken in conservation by local authorities and others, and the opportunities offered by various special initiatives, such as Community Forests.

English Nature owns one reserve on Mendip – Rodney Stoke – which is part of its National Nature Reserve in Somerset. It also manages Ebbor Gorge for the National Trust.

For details of these contact: Roughmoor, Bishops Hull, Taunton TA1 5AA; Tel 01823-283211.

Somerset Wildlife Trust has fourteen reserves on Mendip, totalling over 740 acres, some of which are open to the public. Others require permits for various reasons, such as breeding birds or flowering plants at certain times of year.

For details of locations and permits contact: Fyne Court, Broomfield, Bridgwater TA5 2EQ; Tel: 01823-451587, where you will be sure of a helpful reception.

The Wildlife Trust, Bristol, Bath and Avon: This Trust, with its long name, only manages one reserve in our area, 220 acre Dolebury Warren, for the National Trust. This splendid limestone grassland and heath is known for its butterflies and rare plants.

For details contact: 32 Jacob's Wells Road, Bristol BS8 1DR.; Tel: 0117-926 5490.

The National Trust owns large parts of Mendip which they either run themselves as nature reserves or contract out to Wildlife Trusts or English Nature. As the Trust gains experience in this field it is managing more reserves itself.

Important reserves and walks include the north side of Cheddar Gorge, Ebbor Gorge, Dolebury Camp, Crook Peak and Wavering Down. All are of special importance as natural history sites, with many rare plants and invertebrates, and are SSSIs.

For further information contact: Eastleigh Court, Warminster, Wiltshire; Tel: 01985-847777.

Mendip Society: A most important influence on development in the area and deeply concerned with its history and conservation in the broadest sense. The Society has been particularly active in the fight against the potentially damaging further development of quarrying in the area.

For details of membership and aims contact: Mendip House, 31 Silver Street, Cheddar, Somerset BS27 3LE.

A Piece of Old Mendip

One of the Somerset Wildlife Trust's most important acquisitions has been the traditionally-managed, 86 acre, herb-rich pasture-land of Chancellor's Farm, near Priddy. To find out more about this vital part of the Somerset Wildlife Trust's activities on Mendip I talked to Jan Boyd who has responsibility for conservation on the farm. She walked me round the buildings and surrounding fields explaining with great enthusiasm why the place is so important.

Chancellor's Farm was finally leased by the Somerset Wildlife Trust from the Ministry of Defence in 1990, though they had been interested in the site since the early 1980s. The stumbling block had been that, while the Trust's main interest was in protecting the unique hay meadows, the buildings threatened to be a considerable drain on funds. Eventually, a deal was completed and the Trust was able to go ahead with its plans.

The great attraction of the place is that it is one of the very few parts of Mendip which has been farmed at low intensity in the traditional manner, without chemicals or the use of much machinery, since the Middle Ages, preserving a wonderful mix of herbage. Indeed, much of the farm has never been ploughed in its known history.

An estate existed at Priddy in Saxon times and appears intermittently from the 1200s as one of the estates of the Bishop of Bath and Wells, but in later times, as with much other local land, it passed to the Tudway Estate. In 1934 part of the Estate was bought by the Ministry of Defence for use as a rifle range; they also purchased the surrounding areas, from which the public was excluded for security and safety reasons. Chancellor's Farm came into this 'buffer' zone. The Territorial Army is still active there when the red flag is flying, making it necessary to organise parties of visitors by appointment only.

The tenants who farmed Chancellor's in the early 1930s were the Watts family – father, son and two daughters. When the father died, the son carried on with his sisters, remaining until retirement in 1987.

After this general outline, I asked about the history of the place.

"The first actual record of a dwelling was on a map dated 1570. This took the form of a sketch rather like a children's drawing of a house, labelled 'Chaunselers howse at thende of dey wey'."

"So there is no doubt it is old. But have you any idea where the name came from?"

"Well, there are two theories and you take your pick. 'Chancellor' could be either the Chancellor of Wells Cathedral, or the Chancellor of the Diocese, one of the Bishop's chief legal officers. The other view is that it could simply be the surname of a sixteenth/seventeenth century landowner or tenant around the time of the Reformation. There are several gravestones with the name Chancellor in Priddy churchyard. But there are links also with Glastonbury – as there are all over these parts.

"For instance, the lead cross found in the tomb of Arthur and Guinivere, when the monks opened it in the presence of Edward I, was preserved after the dissolution of the Abbey, but then vanished in the eighteenth century. An American scholar has spent the last few years trying to trace it, believing there may be a connection with the farm, but it seems tenuous. Incidentally, there are two Bronze Age burial mounds on the site, giving links to much older times"

"Tell me more about the buildings."

"Parts are ancient, the oldest being the farm proper, the stable and the barn in the stackyard. The dairy was added later, linking the house to the

111

stable. The older parts of the buildings are seventeenth century, though some of the beams in the dairy, intricately carved on both sides, are from the fifteenth century. The barn is an example of a traditional threshing barn, with raised floor and opposite doors to blow away the chaff."

"What sort of a farm was it then?"

"As far as is known it has always been a working farm. Historians say that when this last building was put up it was an extremely modern layout, using the latest agricultural methods of the time. This compares oddly with its last phase as a farm, when it was an example of the oldest traditional methods, long superseded elsewhere in the country."

Jan Boyd at Chancellor's Farm.

She laughed at the comparison and went on,

"In 1760 it was a mixed farm, with oats, pigs, sheep and cattle and so it continued until before the last war, when it specialised in dairying, and its

Cheddar cheese had quite a reputation in the area. Then, in1952, its milk licence was withdrawn by the Ministry as there was no mains water. This was piped into the dairy soon afterwards, but by then the family had switched to beef. The mains water was never led into the farmhouse or other buildings."

"These people sound an eccentric lot. Tell me more about them."

"Yes, they were unusual. Mr. Watts farmed the place in the mid-1930s, helped by his son Grantly, and two unmarried daughters who took over when he died. The family had a love of the old ways of doing things, a dislike of money and kept themselves to themselves. They lived extremely simply, leaving money and a note in a hole in a boundary wall for suppliers, collecting water from two fields away with a yoke and buckets, and using home-grown wood widely and eeffectively. Hedgerow trees supplied firewood, kindling and all the raw material they needed for fencing and other maintenance.

"They had a large dairy herd up to the war years, then were made to plough two, or possibly three, fields during that period, but managed to retain most of it as permanent pasture, which it remains to this day. The plough ground was re-seeded with grass as soon as it was allowed and reverted to flower-rich meadow sooner than might be expected. This was due to their practice of feeding hay, full of seeds from the meadow, directly
to cattle out in the fields. They used horses for ploughing but bought their only mechanical aid, a tractor, after the war. They disliked modern methods of farming and never used artificial fertiliser. Because their needs were so simple the farm continued to provide a living."

Jan looked round the grasslands as if to emphasise the point.

"They continued dairying until 1950, then went in for beef for a while, finally giving up active farming in 1970. They were an amazing family.

"There are many stories about the people who lived in the house in the past, with its remote and freezing location on the top of the exposed Mendips. Some are said to have coated themselves with grease at the start of winter, putting on a leather garment until the warmer weather returned, while children were sewn into their clothes."

"What a fascinating history, but what about the place itself, now you have come to terms with it?"

"The farm had three rooms upstairs and three downstairs, with walls 25 inches thick. It is laid out on the lines of a traditional Somerset longhouse; there was a range in an outside room and copper boilers in the dairy for heating water. Some things were arranged most ingeniously: whey from the dairy passed down a trough to the shed, some distance away, where the pigs were kept and calves reared. But, as I said, the house had no water. There was no electricity, gas or telephone and there was a two-seater privy still in use to the end. That was how we found it.

"Now it has been transformed, though retaining the character and nature of the place. Kate Lawrence, Mendip Hills Officer for the Trust, lives in the farmhouse with her family and uses it for her office and work rooms, while the dairy has been done up as accommodation for six volunteers. They arrived after university to get practical experience on conservation work. Others who live locally may also join in as volunteers, adding to the labour force. Without these people it would be impossible to deal with this project or make sense of running the many Mendip reserves."

We walked on round the buildings. The East Barn is now an excellent meeting place, interpretation and education centre. Eventually it will be equipped with a computer and microscopes, and will hold the Len Cram library of reference books donated by his widow, but expanded to bring in the latest works as the years go on. Len, who died in 1992, was a prominent member of the Mendip Hills area for the Trust, as well as past-President of the Mendip Society, and much respected for his long and practical knowledge of the area and its wildlife and flora.

The farm is designated an SSSI by English Nature, and the management plan has to be approved by them. The farm has also been entered into the 'Country Stewardship' scheme, in conjunction with a neighbouring farm, and obtains a grant for dry stone walling and to help continue managing the place in traditional, low-intensity ways.

There are some fascinating features on the farm. Perhaps the most interesting of these are the ponds out in the fields. When the Trust first came these were all silted up and there was a deal of damage to stonework. They have now been cleared and repaired into sound working order. They are traditional Mendip dew-ponds where, by clever design, one pond serves either one, two or four fields. The ponds are lined with clay and slope into the centre where the field boundary walls cross, with natural seepage equalising water levels. A four field pond will have a cross of walls separating the animals in each pasture. The water comes only from winter rains or the many Mendip mists.

The soil is unexpected in this huge area of limestone because there is a layer of wind-born loess from eastern Europe, three to four feet deep, making the soil neutral to slightly acidic. The main part of the farm has no surface water as springs and streams run deep underground in the limestone skeleton. The farm well is twenty feet deep, tapping into one of these streams. However, there is a small part of the farm on the other side of the main road where there is a stream, although it becomes more of a marsh in the summer. A well has been dug in the bed of this and supplies clear water throughout the worst drought.

This curious topsoil, the nature of the countryside and the way it has been farmed in a low intensity manner, have retained a profusion of flowers and herbs in the sward. In spring it is covered in Bluebells, presenting a picture such as few people can remember nowadays. It is this profusion which is unique, as well as the variety of the herbage, rather than numbers of rarities. Nevertheless, there are some interesting plants; these include six types of orchid: Common and Heath-spotted, Fragrant, Green-winged, Twayblade and Early Purple. There are two rare ferns, Adder's tongue and Moonwort, while the fields are mauve with Meadow Saffron in the autumn, an amazing sight.

Devil's Bit Scabious grows in profusion in the damper parts, its presence leading to the reintroduction of the very rare Marsh Fritillary Butterfly, under licence from English Nature. Seven adults have been seen flying, so this may be the start of a colony. The rare Great Crested Newt breeds in one of the ponds.

A Corncrake has been heard, Snipe and Jacksnipe are found in the fields, while Whimbrel and Curlew call in Spring and Redstarts breed. Kestrels, Buzzards and four commoner Owls are to be seen, while Badgers and Foxes roam the fields, with a good Hare, Weasel and Stoat population, but the raison d'être of the reserve is the variety and profusion of its flora. Some fields hold 32 species of grass and flowers, an unusual number these days.

The Trust was approached by a commercial firm about supplying some of its meadow seed for sale. A special harvester was hired from a nearby Trust, permission obtained from English Nature and seeds successfully harvested. It is good to think that some of that natural mixture will be growing elsewhere and giving as much pleasure in its new location.

I left, after a sweeping look across the farm with its stone walls, matur trees and green meadows, feeling happy that it was in good hands. This place of ancient history and traditional farming is at least safe for the next few years and, hopefully, for the foreseeable future.

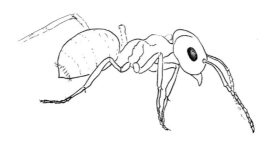

Recently restored Smitham Chimney, once used for lead smelting.

6 Beneath the Ground: Minerals and Caves

While agriculture has certainly played its part, and will continue to do so into the foreseeable future, Mendip has always been most notable for the minerals and rocks found under the ground. Since pre-history man has dug greedily into and beneath the surface, with mining a major industry during the past thousand years, but now defunct. Quarrying stone has taken over in recent years as a big money earner for the county, although its history, too, goes back many centuries.

Controversy has followed these practices over the years, with mine raiding parties in the Middle Ages, the law declaring parts as no-go areas a hundred years or so ago and now much concern about the scale of quarrying and the effect on Mendip's vital water supplies.

Mendip is a harsh area which has always produced equally tough people to exploit its resources; their natural successors must surely be those who spend their weekends underground, exploring the many caves for which the area is famous.

Lead, Silver and Gold

Remains of Iron Age smelting have been found over many parts of Mendip, indicating an industry as important as the subsequent, more famous, lead mining. Unfortunately, the very nature of mining destroys its own traces as later generations work over the same ground. Although Mendip lead was famous in Roman times, it is impossible to pinpoint even one mining shaft as either Iron Age or Roman, so the discovery of relics has helped greatly in establishing details. Leaden objects, including weights for fishing nets, have been found on the sites of both Glastonbury and Meare Lake Villages; it is reasonable to assume the metal came from nearby.

The first documented evidence comes from Leland, the inveterate traveller and recorder of Henry VIII's day, of a pig of Roman lead being ploughed up near Wookey Hole in the 1540s. The official emperor's stamp on it places the date at AD49. The first pig of lead which was not 'lost' or melted down is now in the British Museum; it was discovered in 1853 and, again by its inscription, has been dated at AD49. Other pigs, which must have been dropped while in transit to south coast ports, are now in local museums, together with an exciting find in 1956 at Green Ore. This settlement was of a more basic nature than Charterhouse, but interesting to following generations because it was not mined extensively later. The four pigs discovered there appeared to have been hidden and were in perfect condition. Further finds of Roman coins and artefacts at such places as Priddy, Chewton Mendip and East Harptree also provide clues to Roman occupation.

The landscape at Charterhouse indicates the workings of Romano-British miners but it was not until the nineteenth century that these were investigated. From cottagers nearby came details of coins found in gardens but unfortunately, although the area was checked several times, very sketchy records were made. However, modern aerial photographs of this valley reveal the fascinating outlines of a small town which must have been remarkably industrial in its day.

Lead from Mendip was one of the most valuable commodities found by the Romans. By using a method known as cupellation, they extracted silver, which analysis has shown to be reasonably plentiful among the copper, antimony and tiny traces of gold in the ore. Lead melted in the open air oxidises quickly without affecting any silver, so reasonable quantities can be removed quite easily. It is not known exactly how the Romans smelted the lead and certainly, by the slag left behind, it is obvious that they did not try to extract every ounce. In the last century it became possible to re-smelt by taking silver from Roman refuse, indicating that the ore was so plentiful they preferred to work roughly and rapidly.

With the departure of the Romans, evidence of Mendip lead mining becomes uncertain for several centuries. It is reasonable to assume that some work continued, but there is no mention of it in Domesday Book, nor references during the Saxon and Danish conquests.

It was in 1189 that a Charter was granted by Richard I to the Bishop of Bath and his successors, allowing mining rights wherever they could find lead on their lands in Somerset. This is not to say that mining did not already exist, as it most probably did, merely that a royal sanction for it was being conferred. A further Charter was granted by Henry III in 1235, specifically permitting Jocelin, Bishop of Bath, to dig at Hidun in the King's

Forest of Mendip 'for iron and every other kind of mine'. It would seem there was a royal prerogative controlling mining on any land, but it was not a very profitable business, the Bishops deriving considerably higher revenues from pasture.

The main landowners – the Bishop, Charterhouse and the owners of Harptree and Chewton – became the Lords Royal, keepers of the four mineries at Charterhouse, Priddy and Smitham Hill at Harptree. These each had their own smelting furnaces, water supplies for sieving impurities from the ore, and tax collectors.

Burrington Combe, one of the great limestone outcrops of the region.

With the reign of Elizabeth I, Mendip mines really came into their own. Inevitable conflict must have broken out among the men digging close together in these rich ore-bearing areas. The sixteenth/seventeenth century mining code laid down strict rules for making a claim. After applying for a licence, the prospective miner stood waist-deep in his hole; throwing his pickaxe in either direction, he was granted rights within the distance they reached. He took the extracted ore to be smelted at the nearest minery. Some were 'free-miners' who paid a royalty of ten per cent, known as lot-lead, to the owner of the land; others were employed by a wealthy land-lord, or possibly the bishop, either of whom might have been attracted by the opportunity to make money from the mines. Certainly, it is true that however rich his employer became, after working all his life in the mines, a man could retire in penury.

Detailed records, now preserved at the Waldegrave Estate Office, show that the lot-lead returns paid to the Lord of the Manor at Chewton Liberty between 1608 and 1614 were generally between twenty and thirty tons each half year; output then fell somewhat but fluctuated wildly from around eight tons in 1659 to over fifty-five in 1662. Miners' names were also written on these twice-yearly accounts, showing a rise within a few years from about ten workers to fifty. Even allowing for the reputation of some land-reeves for defrauding their lords, while possibly some miners did the same to the land-reeves, this was undoubtedly the peak of production.

It was during this time that German miners introduced divining rods. They are first mentioned as being used in the Welsh silver mines, followed by references to 'dowsing', the West Country word for divining. This is now more popularly associated with searches for water, although it is be-lieved that metal divining came first. While more educated people were highly cynical of the use of such methods to find ore, the miners themselves had implicit faith in their rods, using them until about 1872. An interesting story tells how a Mr. Capper Pass and friend issued a dowsing challenge to some miners in a Mendip village, possibly Gurney Slade. A test was set up in the village inn, using hats and handkerchiefs, some of which covered coins placed on the floor. Mr. Pass and his friend decided that, while these trials were inconclusive, some results were inexplicable. They conceded that possibly a subconscious perception could pass through some miners' bodies. No-one has yet come up with a better explanation, unless you choose not to believe it at all.

Mining for lead or other metals took place over the whole of Mendip, from Bleadon in the west across to Binegar and Croscombe. These excava-tions can be seen clearly in places where the surface looks rough and bro-ken, the grubby ground, or 'gruffy'ground, as it is known, giving Mendip its unique and characteristic appearance. The gruffs were the mine shafts, which were about a hundred feet deep and sometimes lined with unmortared masonry. Where lead was close to the surface, shallow grooves were cut, perhaps extending for a hundred yards or so, and giving the name 'groovers' to the miners. Sometimes there were a series of small pits in lines across the fields. The deeper shafts have been filled in, but occasionally injuries have been caused to both humans and animals where covers have given way.

West Harptree today. Manor and Church.

Once a vein was opened up, the miner worked it by extracting ore from between the surrounding limestone rocks. This empty tunnel became known as a 'leer', one of the most famous of which is Lamb's Leer near West Harptree. This was a very large cave originally broken into by miners in the middle of the seventeenth century. Hearing this news, Mr. Beaumont, a resident of nearby Ston Easton very bravely decided to explore the 'great vault', taking six miners with him. They found their way along the vertical shaft and passages until they came to the Great Chamber. In spite of bribes of double salaries, all the miners refused to go down, which is not surprising since their candles were totally inadequate to penetrate the darkness. Unwilling to abandon his quest, Mr. Beaumont tied a cord round himself and persuaded them to lower him down gently. Soon he could not touch any rocks around him to act as a guide and began spinning round. Where most of us would probably have shouted to be hauled up at once, he called to the miners to let him down as fast as they could. Luckily, there was no water when he arrived at the bottom of the cavern, which he estimated to be about twenty fathoms high. Undaunted, he untied the cord and searched around, to his delight finding some good lead ore at one end. In due course, he had a ladder made for easy descent and persuaded miners to work out the ore, which lasted for some considerable time.

However, in spite of being documented and living in local legend, the cave appears to have become inaccessible sometime in the eighteenth century. It was not until 1873 that a fresh search was instigated. A company which had leased a large part of that area of Mendip for prospecting decided it might be profitable to reopen Lamb Leer. It took thirty-seven unsuccessful borings before, in 1880, they re-entered the cavern which had been closed for almost two centuries. Unable to mine further, it was opened to the public for a while, but fell into disuse until the generation of 'real' cavers arrived on the scene at the turn of the century.

Miners' Arms, reflecting the old interests of the area.

After reaching its peak, the production of lead began to slide downhill around 1670, mainly due to the easily accessible ore being worked out. There may well have been plenty more at a lower level, but this was difficult to reach, especially with regular flooding at any time of the year. Even the later use of machinery could not keep the water completely at bay. However, certain pockets of mining continued on Mendip, but its demise was hastened in 1825 when the protective duty on imported lead was reduced, which affected even the higher quality ore found in other English mines.

Although mining for lead-ore became extinct around 1850, both before and after that date for many years a large amount of metal was extracted from the refuse left behind. In spite of being re-smelted at least once before, with the use of more sophisticated machinery it was still possible to extract lead. It was during this brief revival in the 1860s that the first Cornish miners arrived on the scene. Nicholas Ennor, a mining engineer, set up 'Buddles' – the round pits in which the slag was prepared for smelting. There was insufficient running water for buddling at Priddy, but at Velvet Bottom, Charterhouse and Chewton Mineries considerable resmelting of the black slag took place, continuing until the 1870s.

It is no surprise to learn that lead-poisoning was a grave hazard to health, for both humans and animals. This was particularly the case for farms and houses near centres of ore-washing. Cattle became 'minedered' when their drinking water was infected or after eating grass on which the contents of the smoke, laden with lead vapour, had fallen. Strangely enough, other animals, such as sheep, are not affected, but the lead builds up in the kidneys and livers of cattle before affecting the brain, causing a distressing death.

The miners themselves had to face the prospect of reduced life expectancy, especially those who came into contact with fumes when working the furnaces. Living in remote areas, generally under harsh conditions, it must have been an insecure and hard life, so it is small wonder they had an unenviable reputation for savagery and depravity. At least, this was according to Hannah More and her sister, who felt they were 'even beyond the people of Cheddar'. However, we have to remember that, apart from the high moral standards set by these two ladies, violence can be caused by lead in the brain. We do know that many of the men had great spirit, fighting bravely, if hopelessly, at the Battle of Sedgemoor; and in 1797 all the able-bodied men of Shipham marched to Bristol, prepared to fight against the French after their invasion at Fishguard.

Pollution affected quite a wide area. Fish died in the Axe down in the valley and folks in Cheddar complained that the lead works at Charterhouse had reduced their stream to a semi-muddy state. A long running disagreement arose between Nicholas Ennor, by that time the proprietor of St. Cuthbert's Lead Works near Priddy, and Mr. Hodgkinson, whose Mill at Wookey Hole manufactured very fine paper. It was claimed that the practice of buddling ore in the streams, which emerge two miles further down at Wookey, contaminated the water. In 1863 the case came to court, with trenchant arguments on both sides. Finally, judgement was given for

Mr. Hodgkinson, stating that he was entitled to expect pure water and, indeed, polluting matter had been allowed to flow into the stream.

Some ten years after this came the closure of St. Cuthbert's, only to be reopened in the mid 1880s. In spite of fluctuating market prices, it remained in almost continuous production until finally closing in 1908.

Calamine

Calamine was found extensively in the Shipham and Rowberrow areas of Mendip and was mined from the reign of Elizabeth I to the end of the Napoleonic Wars. Together with copper, the zinc contained in calamine was used in the production of brass, and for a while Mendip become one of the main suppliers to the brass foundries of Europe.

It was in the eighteenth century that production reached its full intensity, providentially taking over from the declining lead industry and providing fresh work in the area. Interestingly, in the 1790s very pure calamine was found at Mells, which is some distance away, but the main supplies came from the Shipham and Rowberrow areas where the villages were completely taken over by small mines. At the end of the eighteenth century there was talk of 'upwards of 100 mines, in the streets, in the yards and in the very houses of Shipham'. These little cottages sprang up everywhere as mining claims increased, giving the village its unique honeycomb appearance, unlike any other on Mendip.

This calamine was supplied mainly to the Bristol Brass Wire Company, described as 'perhaps the most considerable brass house in all Europe'. Over four-hundred men were employed in mining at its peak but, inevitably, the trade declined and by the end of the Napoleonic Wars mining for calamine had ceased. As with the lead, it is extremely unlikely ever to be seen on the Mendip Hills again.

The effects of the mining may still be seen in a lack of old trees, burnt for fuel or poisoned by the fumes of the ovens. Traces of roughened ground can be found in the area, although most have been lost inside Shipham, which is a flourishing modern village. By contrast the old cottages of Rowberrow, once the same size as its neighbour, have almost vanished.

Calamine made an enormous impact on the area, booming for several decades, only to vanish virtually without trace.

Coal

Coal seams were formed under the Mendip hills some fifty million years ago and they, too, have been exploited. The miners deservedly earned the reputation for being some of the best in the world as they had to work under very difficult conditions. Geological faults, thin seams, awkward coal formations and flooding meant the gradual adoption of new techniques. Added to this was the absence of any proper roads and the hilly conditions in which the coal had to be transported. So the industry progressed only slowly, but by 1750 investors were showing interest and more mines were opening in Somerset.

The remains of coal pits are visible in a number of Mendip villages. The valley of Nettlebridge has mute reminders with its abandoned ruins. Tragically, nearby Vobster suffered two coal mining disasters. The first was in 1773 when four miners were killed after a gas explosion, and a further eleven died in Old Breach Mine in 1800. Perhaps a little unexpectedly, mining was in operation as far back as the reign of Charles II in the picturesque village of Mells.

Coleford's name implies the presence of both coal and water. Its old viaduct still stands, a silent memorial of the far-sighted, but unfortunately unfinished, Dorset and Somerset Canal. This should have been a great asset to the pits for rapid coal transportation eastwards, but funds gave out in 1803. The start of the canal was to have been in another, unexpected, mining village – Stratton-on-the-Fosse now famous for Downside Abbey, not the dirt and bustle of coal.

The beginning of the nineteenth century showed some thirty pits in operation in the whole of Somerset, although there were many problems of transport, draining and ventilation in the Mendip area. The boom period occurred around the middle of the century, with a considerable improvement in miners' conditions, but by the 1890s many pits were exhausted and closing down. The construction of rail links, especially that between Frome and Radstock in 1853, put the final nail in Mendip's coffin, ensuring that Radstock became the hub of coal mining in the area.

It is believed that there are at least eleven million tons of coal still underground.

Rock Quarrying

As long as there has been a need, rock has been hewn from the Mendips. This whale-shaped massif is composed of some of the finest quality hard limestone rock in Britain, becoming a major source of raw material for present-day road building throughout the country. Covering the limestone in parts are caps of a red sandstone, which has a characteristic appearance and has been much-used for building in the region.

Old Red Sandstone and the special conglomerate, Draycott Stone, are found on Iron Age and Roman sites both in and outside the Mendip area, and almost every village has its church using this material. Wells Cathedral owes its mellow beauty to stone from Doulting Quarry and, with the arrival of the Cheddar Valley Line many years later, it was used to build the railway stations. Today, there are only two working quarries supplying under one thousand tons of this special Doulting Stone annually.

Currently there are nine active quarries on Mendip, from which the majority of material goes into road-building, though part of the production is used in concrete blocks and paving slabs. Somerset is the second largest supplier of roadstone in the country.

The great majority of new roads are surfaced with tarmac using crushed rock. The property of limestone is such that, when used as a sub-base in road building, it compacts and matures into a form of concrete, giving added strength. For those who grieve over the scars caused by quarries in this region, it is unfortunate that the Mendips provide one of the country's major deposits of high-quality hard rock, as well as being the nearest supply to parts of the voracious South-East.

At present, over seventeen million tonnes of aggregate are quarried annually, with the amount rising each year. This does not appear to be a great deal but it is frightening to see the crusher gobbling up stone on East Mendip. Here, there is already a hole the size of Cheddar Gorge, which ARC wishes to double over the next twenty years. Permissions were granted before planning came into being in 1948, so there were no safeguards written in. What County Hall clerk would have considered preserving our environment fifty years ago? However, since 1991, quarry operators have had to register Interim Development Orders with the Minerals Planning Authority, giving details of proposed environmental protection. At the time of writing, nineteen are being considered by the Authority.

The Somerset Wildlife Trust pointed out in 1994 that more stone has been dug out of the County since 1960 than in all the previous centuries combined. The Trust went on to advocate the use of top quality Mendip stone for particular uses only, such as the removal of flue-gas in coal-fired power stations, to reduce acid rain. They suggest that recycled stone would be perfectly adequate for most needs. This would kill two birds with one stone by using up unsightly waste products as well as preserving beautiful areas of the countryside. However, Government policy is keeping the price of stone at such an artificially low level that no recycled waste can compete.

Four major companies supply the majority of aggregate and, not unexpectedly, take a different stance, maintaining that there are many misconceptions. Defending extraction from the Mendips, they state that it is uneconomic to use hard rock from Devon and Cornwall, and the sixteen million tonnes taken in 1987 is less than seven per cent of the national production of all aggregates. They consider that the use of recycled products is not economically viable, with the end product unacceptable for many purposes.

Quoting Government policy 'to ensure that the construction industry continues to receive an adequate and steady supply of minerals at the best balance of social, environmental and economic costs,' the organisation stresses that noise and dust pollution are kept as low as possible, with quarry workings landscaped, and environmental codes of practice now being published by some operators.

Although quarry owners say there is an increasing use of rail from Whatley and Torr Quarries, a dip into local newspapers indicates a high degree of concern over heavy lorries travelling through many local villages during the day, only to rattle emptily back at night. With a daily total of nearly 4,000 journeys into and out of the Mendips, this anxiety is hardly surprising, and anyone who has been squeezed against the wall of a pavementless village street by a large truck, laden with stone, will certainly echo this fear.

Of course this argument depends where you stand. For those employed in the industry, quarrying is a major supplier of jobs in this sparsely-inhabited area, providing their bread-and-butter. In 1991, more than seven hundred people were employed directly and around two thousand indirectly, though modernisation has seen a gradual reduction in numbers.

Mendip District Council and Somerset County Council are researching the impact of the quarry industry on the environment, covering archaeology, noise, air quality, wildlife, traffic, access and water.

Fortunately for the Mendips, councillors and even quarry companies are united in condemning as absurd the incredible prediction from forecasters that the figure for stone extraction will rise to about 28 million tonnes per annum by 2006. If correct, the Quarry Policy would mean the disappearance of the Mendips by 2200!

Nunney Castle, a monument to Mendip Stone.

Concerns about the Effects of Quarrying

The steep-sided hills that face the prevaling south-west winds are responsible for Mendip's high rainfall. Add to this the occurrence of aquifers underlying the porous limestone hills, and it can be appreciated how this generous flow supplies thirttewn million litres of water daily to the people of the area, including North Somerset and Bristol. Equally important is the flow which feeds the great wetlands of the Somerset Levels below.

Unfortunately, aggregate quarries and water supplies can make uneasy bed fellows, causing considerable concern over pollution and alterations in the water table. The delicate balance of water underground can be upset drastically by careless boring or attempts to quarry deeper. Pollution from quarrying is known to have occurred at two springs, while a number of others have reduced flows or have dried completely.

Pollution is one thing which can perhaps be remedied, but the effects of reduced water supplies could be catastrophic to the region. Some experts are predicting that immediate plans for deepening quarries will have a serious effect on the water-table. Indeed, they say it is already happening, but that future changes could be much more serious. All this has come to light with plans being put forward to deepen quarries which have reached the end of existing permissions.

Any alteration to the delicate balance of water-flow could lead to permanent damage in the form of reduced domestic water-supplies, lack of water going to the Levels – a major Environmentally Sensitive Area by Government definition – and unknown harm in the systems and caves beneath the ground. It is suggested that this whole question should only be determined after much more thought and research. Commerce wants to continue development, conservationists oppose any extension. Is there some middle way which will maintain employment while minimising damage?

The Caves of Mendip

The Mendip Hills contain some of the finest cave-systems in Britain. The limestone of which they are composed is slightly soluble in water. As rain falls onto the rock it runs into fissures, dissolves these further and eventually penetrates deep down, carving out great caves and passages. All this takes millions of years, although the process is continual and continuing.

Many of the swallet-holes, which lead water beneath the surface, occur at the junction of insoluble red sandstone and limestone. Streams disappear underground, often running hundreds of feet below, carving their way more deeply each year, although this may be almost immeasurable. Where the rock is softer, dissolving occurs more widely, producing the great caverns. These are usually part of a continuing system or underground stream. Some of the original openings were blocked in the last Ice Age, ten thousand years ago, but signs often show where they could be expected. Many cave entrances have been exposed only after extensive digging.

The Mendips have been one of the major British caving regions for nearly a hundred years, providing enthusiasts with a close-knit selection of caves, most of which are only a few minutes' walk from a road.

During the nineteenth century considerable archaeological work was carried out in the area, and in the 1890s caving came into its own as a sporting activity, as opposed to early chance explorations by miners and a few adventurous souls. One of these was Herbert Earnest Balch, 'The Father of Mendip Caving', who spent all his life in Wells. He became interested in archaeology as a teenager, which led him on to exploring and enhancing his knowledge of caves, starting with Wookey Hole. In those early days, while he was being lowered into the dark and unknown depths of the main chamber in Lamb Leer, the rope broke. He fell nearly sixty feet and was knocked unconscious, which could have put an end to his caving career. Luckily it was not too serious, but activities virtually ceased for nearly five years, until the next great thrust in August, 1901, when Balch and a group of friends decided to explore below a swallet close to Priddy church. This was the beginning of true Mendip caving, and of Swildon's Hole, in particular, which to this day is yielding its secrets to persistent cavers and divers.

While Balch was a truly local explorer and writer of many books and articles on caves, thus bringing them very much to wide attention, he was not alone in this pioneering work. In 1903 Dr. Baker, who was born in Somerset but lived in the Derby area, joined Balch's group in an exploration of Eastwater Swallet. Thus began a long career of exploration in which Baker became more active, while Balch took less of a physical part, although continuing to write. They were the forerunners of a number of brave men who pushed their way further and further under the Mendip Hills, leaving a permanent reminder to others in such places as the famous GB Cave (named after two University students, Goddard and Barker, coupled with patriotic sentiments, the find being just after the Second World War); Trat's Temple in Swildon's; Read's Cavern; and Browne's Passage at Stoke Lane Slocker. In November, 1961, quarrying operations opened up a cave which was probably one of the finest in the country. It was named Balch's Cave but, unfortunately, much of it has now been quarried away, destroying its appeal for any serious caver.

Between 1910 and the Second World War a number of clubs were formed, others joined them after 1945, and now there are at least seventy flourishing in the South of England. These clubs adhere to very strict regulations, insisting that it is vital for members to carry clear details of underground routes with them. They are also asked to leave concise, written messages of their planned return times with local cavers who are knowledgeable about conditions on Mendip. Experienced cavers are the most suited to give the best advice about weather conditions and stream-flows, because any changes, such as sudden heavy rain, will not be detected underground until flooding occurs.

Other strict rules apply to caring for the caving environment by avoiding breakages or unnecessary trampling of the area, together with removal of all equipment and litter. As above ground, conservation is a major talking point, trying to ensure that the minimum deterioration is caused when opening up new caves or visiting long established ones. In the past, there has been vandalism with the smashing or stealing of precious formations, but now responsible carers are going to great lengths to create a caring attitude towards these vulnerable places. It is reassuring to discover that among the areas which have caves, seven are classed as Sites of Special Scientific Interest, which should preserve them from any potentially damaging undertakings. It is recognised that caving can cause environmental headaches, and it is not hard to see why when perhaps some five hundred cavers are active within the underground system on any one weekend. Inevitably, this can lead to erosion and problems with litter. A number of landowners are now insisting that entrances to caves on their land are locked, to avoid unauthorised access by non-cavers. They do not wish to be involved in insurance claims from the public or lose animals down holes. Bona fide cavers have access through their Clubs, who hold keys.

Due to the geology of the area, Mendip caves are notable for being steeply sloping; they are seldom deeper than five hundred feet and about a mile or so in length. But within this relatively small area there can be a rich variety of vast caverns, very narrow passages, water splashing down over rock formations and fascinating decorations. Some of the mining, which went on from before Roman times to the middle of the nineteenth century, has broken into the natural caves, adding further interest to explorers. In this area of Mendip the best known are Ochre Mine at Axbridge and Lamb Leer Cavern at West Harptree.

To those of us who dread feeling claustrophobic below tons of earth and rock, with the added fear of becoming stuck, unable to move forward or back, a browse through a Caver's Guide can make compelling, if terrifying, reading. Some of the maps of the bigger caves, with their descriptive names such as Suicide Rift, Horrofices 1 and 2, Stick-in-the-Mud Passage, Agony Crawl, Sewer Passage, Bloody Tight and Black Hole Series, could have us reaching for the whisky bottle. But then, what are we missing? Bertie's Paradise, Icing Flake Chamber, Princess Grotto, Upper Wardour Street, Fairy Cave and Garden of Eden. Maybe we should be heading for the hills, too.

Swildon's Hole at Priddy is the longest cave on Mendip and, being very popular, can get crowded at weekends. It has a high-level range of mainly dry passages but under certain wet conditions part of the cave, including the entrance, can flood, which causes both danger and added excitement to anyone below. Cave maps show the many choices available, to suit various standards of ability from beginner to very experienced; anyone who wants a dip at the Lavatory Pan can crawl along the Wet Way.

The entrance was opened in 1901 by H.E. Balch with a group from Wells

Natural History & Archaeological Society, but it then took thirty-five years to reach one-fifth of the total known area today. The tremendous volume of water descending the forty feet pitch was to hold explorers at bay for twenty years, and was itself washed away in the great flood of July 1968. The many sumps in the cave proved dangerous and impassable for a long while. Sumps sound fascinating. There are over a dozen of them in Swildon's, requiring navigation by experienced divers, many of whom free-dive. It is difficult to imagine actually adding lead weights from the bucket at Sump 2 to a lamp belt. This provides negative buoyancy to get well below the surface of the very cold water, thus dipping beneath bulges in the roof above. Then it is a matter of pulling on the guide line to get through to the next cavern. It must take a great deal of nerve to be the first person to dive and search for a way through to the next cavern, but it is only due to such bravery in taking this calculated risk that these amazing networks have stretched further and further under the Mendips.

A landscape of stone walls and remote farms.

A very good example of this is Wookey Hole, with its passages formed millions of years ago by the River Axe. A great deal of diving has been carried on here, in the 1980s achieving the record of over two-hundred feet for a dive. In 1975 a tunnel was driven from the cliff face to extend the tourist route from the Third to the Ninth Chamber, which had been discovered by divers twenty-seven years earlier, but it is incredible to think that cave divers have opened the system as far as the Twenty-fifth Chamber. We can only wonder what the earliest known inhabitants of the cave in 2BC would make of this, but Wookey Hole always held a fascination, being mentioned by poets in the thirteenth century. One of them, Alexander Pope, is reputed to have committed the unforgivable sin of having some stalactites shot down so that he could use them ornamentally in his own garden. So the caves had already been denuded of some of their beauty by the time they became a popular tourist centre in the eighteenth century.

In common with those first explorers at the start of this century, many of us may think caves are just holes in the ground that can be entered easily, to find a network of passages, large caverns and maybe even the odd lake. This can be far from the truth, with even the entrances to some caves on Mendip being notable for the hours spent digging to open them up. It was not unknown for several abortive attempts to be made in an effort to find a way in, working on assumptions of where water vanished under the soil at swallets. Once underground, hours and hours of digging over many years have been necessary to clear ways through and, on occasions, blasting has been used. In an attempt to get through Sump 1 in Swildon's Hole, large quantities of gelignite were packed in one Saturday in March, 1934. This did not do the job properly so another effort was made the following day. Unfortunately for the cavers, Sump 1 is nearly underneath Priddy Church and it is reputed that the explosion caused sufficient shock waves to lift the congregation into the air – certainly enough to distract their attention from the service and lead them to have indignant words with the cavers when they returned to the surface. But it was worthwhile because the blasting turned out to have been a success. This was the start of cave-diving, although the equipment was unbelievably primitive at first, consisting of garden hose pipe, tubing from a bicycle frame and some tin cans. Two months before the Priddy 'earthquake', at the first blasting attempt on Sump 1, Grahame Balcombe, who actually was a member of the Northern Cavern and Fell Club in the Yorkshire area, is reported to have worked for thirty-seven hours underground. This is a very long period but lengthy expeditions, with their necessary transportation of equipment and passage explorations, were, and still are, quite common.

In 1938 technology entered the arena in the form of a geo-electric survey by Professor Lionel Palmer, who hoped to find a large chamber in Lamb Leer. This involved measurements of an electric current passed through the ground. Resistance increases over a cave where the air is more unyielding than the surrounding rock. It seemed likely that there was a large cavern close to the already known Main Chamber and near the surface, but the Second World War put an almost complete stop to any caving for the next few years. A further survey with improved instruments was undertaken in 1957, which appeared to confirm the existence of what had hopefully been named Palmer's Chamber but, in spite of hours of exploration, so far this has remained elusive.

As far back as 1135, there were tales of a 'lost cave' at Cheddar. The fact that the river which emerges at the bottom of Cheddar Gorge bears similarities to that at Wookey Hole lent credence to this. Richard Gough, a name synonymous with caves in Cheddar, attempted to follow the river upstream by blasting a passage, which only succeeded in breaking nearby windows, it is said. Repeated diving attempts, diggings and searching finally proved successful in 1985 when the Main River cave was discovered by R. Stevenson, a cave diver. During the next few years some three thousand feet of cave passage were explored, revealing fine river passages and vast chambers. Even so, surely there must be many passages and caves under the Mendip Hills which still wait to show their treasures to future explorers.

Cheddar Gorge and Priddy between them have something like fourteen major caves, the latter containing St. Cuthbert's Swallet, which is the second longest and undoubtedly the most complex cave system on Mendip. They are closely followed by nine major ones at both Burrington Combe and Stoke St. Michael, with a further eight major ones at Charterhouse. With still more caves in the area, if you have ever felt a sneaking desire to crawl, wriggle through or just gaze at this fascinating network beneath your feet, why not make a start? There is certainly plenty of choice and a whole new world to enter and explore.

7 People of Mendip

In trying to come to terms with what is going on in Mendip, and the changes seen over a lifetime, we decided to talk to people who have known the area all their lives and with experience of particular aspects of life on the hills.

Decisions on activities or specialities were not difficult: farming, strawberry-growing, caving and, finally, conservation and natural history, seemed to take in the prime areas except quarrying, covered elsewhere. Finding the right people was another matter. We were lucky in being directed towards those whom we interviewed, all very much part of the scene and with long memories. But they represent only a tiny fraction of the experiences of people who make their living from Mendip or just plain enjoy it.

Bill Small, Mendip Farmer

The Smalls farm on the thin limestone soil of western Mendip, near Charterhouse, with most of their land at between nine hundred and one thousand feet. It is approached down a long track with sweeping views north over Mendip, past a windbreak of very large trees. It must be one of the finest entrances to a farm and brings home the remoteness of the location in former days, before the motor car shrunk distances so much.

There are two houses, a new one and the original farmhouse, together with buildings which take up a considerable area. The house is substantial, built in grey limestone, springing out of the ground as if it was living rock.

I parked in the yard and was greeted by Mr Small, who took me to sit in a room with a splendid inglenook fireplace. The room has that lived-in look of the working farm – comfortable, with people coming in and out during the evening, going out again to look at the animals and the never-ending jobs which are part of a busy farm.

I asked how large the farm was and what was its history.

Mr Small looked up at his son, James, who works with them, "What were the figures you worked out last week?"

"930 acres, of which we own just over 650. The rented ground includes a deal of conservation land; National Trust and Somerset Trust, with whom we work closely. Because of our size we are able to fit in with their special requirements by moving animals around."

Bill Small, Mendip farmer.

Mr Small continued, "My brother John and I took over the farm as partners thirty years ago, with 330 acres. The rest has been built gradually over the years and suits our type of farming – sheep in the main – which need a good acreage to make sense. My grandfather had eleven farms on Mendip but these became split up among his children and grandchildren who have had to build it up again. Now the partnership has been widened to include our two wives and my son."

"How do you farm and what stock do you keep?"

"The main business is sheep. We keep a permanent flock of 2,000 speckled Welsh ewes, with a total of up to 4,000 during summer after lambing. We breed mainly speckled cross blue-faced Leicester ewe-lambs for sale as breeding stock to other farms, while the wethers are sold for meat. Mendip is well suited to this business. We also keep 250 or so beef cattle as sucklers and stores, for sale to lowland farms for fattening on. All our land is down to grass nowadays, much as permanent pasture or long leys, and we make both hay and silage for winter feeding."

"Has this changed much over the years?"

"Oh yes. We grew between 100 and 300 acres of corn in those days, kept a flock of some 300 ewes and a few cattle. Eventually, in common with many in this area, we were defeated by the mildew on cereals. The high rainfall made it impossible to grow corn economically on this soil. It is possible to spray against this disease but the costs outweigh the benefits and you cannot compete against those without our particular problems. The acreage of cereals is much reduced on Mendip nowadays, as more farmers realise what they are up against. We milked up to 1963, then it snowed from Boxing Day on and we were shut off until March 14th – I remember those dates as if they were yesterday. The water was pumped up from below and then the pump split and the electricity failed. This was the final straw; we loaded up the cattle, after driving them over the snow which covered the walls, took them to market and that was the end."

"Do you employ anyone on the farm now?"

"No, though we use contractors for a number of operations which used to be considered just a part of a farmer's work. Contractors do the bailing, dipping and shearing now. It is interesting to see the changes taking place; when we started all shearing was done by us and our neighbours. This last year the sheep were sheared by two Norwegians and a fellow from the Falkland Islands! It certainly opens your mind to the outside world."

"Do you have a barn for them to sleep in?"

"No, none of that Australian stuff. We put them up in the house and feed them. They're good company." Mrs Small broke in, "They don't so much sleep in the beds as on them," with a smile, "and they have large appetites."

"It is still to some extent communal," Mr Small said, "The shearers stay three or four days and do our own sheep plus those of some neighbours, who drive their sheep in here. It takes a couple of days to do the dipping and again we bring in three neighbouring flocks of sheep as well."

He paused a moment, "Although we co-operate over this, it is not the same as when we first started. Then everything depended on farmers working together. All the major farm events involved you and your neighbours getting together and doing the job as fast as possible. We knew everyone really well and depended on each other. This has gradually vanished, although we may get together to make the best use of a contractor's time. In those days we were the workers. Your neighbours helped out, then you in turn gave up time to help them, whether it was shearing, dipping, haymaking or whatever. Now we have to be bigger to make a living and somehow time is much shorter, so we pay others to do some of the work, leaving us to concentrate on planning and the day-to-day activities."

"Everyone seems to be in a rush nowadays," I said, "Why?"

"Part is the need to produce more to make the same living, part is all the paperwork which swamps us. Now we have to become involved in more and more enterprises to keep going. Apart from the farming, my brother and I drive cattle lorries, carrying our own livestock and those of others to market or slaughterhouses. This has grown over the years and we have a large artic. as well as a smaller vehicle.

"No, we don't go abroad. The driving has to fit in with the rest of the farmwork; most of our journeys are not much further than Bristol. Then my brother's wife does bed and breakfast, while we have a number of regulars who come down for a few days for a break from London and other cities. They seem to like our way of life and the air up here.

"As for the paperwork, James went to Cannington Farm Institute on Day Release and has come out with a good clear idea of what is needed and how to deal with it."

James chipped in, "We now have everything on computer and believe we are more in charge of our activities, but then you must be, with the pressures nowadays."

I asked when water and electricity came to Mendip.

"The first water came up to the farm in 1939, by way of a hydram from below. Lady Annerley owned the water rights in the area and when she died she left a will giving us the first 250 gallons a day free, in compensation for water taken to fill the Cheddar water tanks. And so it remains to this day – a more valuable concession each year. 1963 brought the first water pumped by electricity, even though it failed in the bad frosts. Electricity first came to the farm in the winter of 1963."

"You mentioned horses earlier. When did you stop using them, or do you still?"

"We still have horses on the farm and up to only a few years ago we used to herd sheep with them in some of the further-off points on the hill, but now we have a 'quad', a four wheel scramble-type motorbike, which has made life much easier. The dogs used to run alongside the horses when we were travelling and arrived worn-out. Now they hop onto the quad and are completely fresh when they are needed. A quad keeps going where animals tire themselves out. But we have not lost touch with horses, we still have a sponsored ride on the farm, hold an annual horse-show and a young farmers' dance in the house. All this raises money for local charities – some £35,000 in the last ten years."

"What sort of horses were they and what other jobs did they do?"

"They were Cobs crossed with Shires, not great hefty animals but sturdy and with good pulling power. Up to 1963 they were used for a variety of hauling and cultivating jobs round the farm, as well as for riding. In the last few years of that period their main job was pulling timber for the forestry people, particularly the first thinnings inside the forest, where a horse could get in the narrower and trickier spots. But horses had a hard life and so did those who managed them. At lambing time a horse might stay forty-eight hours in shafts, as the family worked shifts out on the hill, and could take fifteen hours to rake up one of the large forty or fifty acre fields of the area. One horse managed to rake ninety acres one year. They were hard days then and the tractor and quad have taken away a deal of drudgery. Mark you, we still have one working Cob which is used for recovering dead animals from awkward places."

I asked him what was the background to his family, it sounded so interesting.

"Great grandfather started Batscombe Quarry. He had a dozen horses working on the roads and needed material for surfacing. He had 12 children also, which perhaps made him anxious to keep his business going, and he was one of the first to grow strawberries commercially in Cheddar Valley. My Uncle Reg put the first road up from Burrington Combe and only died three years ago, which gives an idea of how much can change in one lifetime. My father rented ground to start farming in 1931 and finally bought his farm in 1961. Incidentally, another uncle built St Hugh's Chapel, on the site of an old miner's meeting house at Charterhouse."

Mrs Small's father ended up locally after many years in Bristol working for Willetts the corn-merchants, inspecting cargoes of grain and cattle-cake coming into the docks. Finally he came to Mendip to manage Wellington Farm, high above Cheddar Gorge, for his firm. This was where Pat met Bill, when horse-raking a field.

I went on to ask what were the main changes Bill had noticed in their years of farming, apart from the move out of cereals.

"It's everyone having transport. This has removed all the services we enjoyed when it was much more cut off. When we were first married milk was delivered in the area three days a week, groceries and bread three times, the butcher called weekly and so did the fishmonger. Now no tradesmen call apart from the postman and even he has trouble when it is snowing. The other is that we see no reps nowadays, unless there is some specific reason. Several used to call each week years ago, selling cattle-feed, fertiliser or chemicals. Then all the small corn-merchants were taken over or closed down and now you have to take the initiative and phone in an order.

Life is emptier without them, you don't hear what is going on in the area unless you get out and about in your own vehicle."

So, paradoxically, it seems that Mendip was less lonely when it was more remote.

"Does being here have its own problems in other ways?"

"Yes, some of the land round here is poisoned with lead from the old workings. We lost a couple of cattle last week from this. There is nothing you can do, it is a part of living in the area."

"The house looks interesting, has it any history?" I asked.

"It was built in the middle of the last century, though some form of house has been here for much longer. When we dug out the inglenook there were four different fireplaces behind it, ending with one of the old beehive type, and there is an Adam fireplace in one of the bedrooms, which must have been installed later; as a result it is now a Listed Building."

He paused, "But the real interest lies much earlier. Warren Farm Cave was excavated some years ago and found to contain so many bodies that it has been kept sealed. There are a great many skeletons down there, some dating from before the Romans and found to have leprosy, others more recent, from the fourteenth century. One of the bodies had an axe-head buried in its skull. The cave also held Auroch bones – the prehistoric ox better known for its origins in ancient Russia. We also have a number of other interesting features on the land we farm; three tumuli, a Roman and an Iron Age Fort, as well as the lead mining for which the area round Charterhouse is famous."

Mr Small then went to a cupboard and pulled out a box holding a number of flint arrowheads and knives found on the farm and, the pièce de résistance, a beautiful bronze axehead discovered when ploughing some years ago. The flint weapons were sharp enough to cut easily, while the axehead was beautifully cast, with sockets to fit the ends of the handle before binding and with a clean surface finish. Apart from a green bloom it looked as good as the day it was made. It was strange looking at it, to think of people making it nearby some four thousand years ago.

We moved on from there to some of the characters of the area.

"There have been plenty of those, for character often goes with hard work and a hard life. Way back one farmer went down to sell some grain in Cheddar, celebrated on the proceeds and was arrested for being drunk in charge of a horse, perhaps he fell off in front of the constable! Come to that there were the horses. Some could be sent off through the gate and would make their way down to Cheddar with a load, wait to be re-loaded, then make their own way back up to the farm, all without a driver. One of our sows used to be pushed through the gate at the right time, would walk down to another farm where they had a boar, be served, and then make her way up again. Our own house-cow had the same habit, but of course the roads were empty in those days.

"Nobody had much money when we were lads. If we wanted a night out in Cheddar we would shoot or snare some rabbits – there were thousands around in those days – and sell them when we got there, on foot of course. The farm used to ferret or shoot some three or four hundred a week. When the rabbits vanished yields of corn rose steeply, it is difficult to realise how many there were in those times before myxomatosis. Now Cheddar is really geared to the visitors. Priddy is our local centre and very good it is. Everyone in the village works hard at a good social life and the village hall is booked solidly ahead. Mendip is a good place to live and work, for all the changes we have seen, and newcomers to the area seem to try to keep this so."

David Sheldon, Strawberry Grower

David Sheldon has been in the business all his life but retired in 1989, following a bad accident to his wife, Hazel, who was shot in the ankle by bandits when they were travelling in the Burma triangle some six years ago. She has had the ankle fused but it still gives her pain and has debilitated her considerably. As a result of this Mr Sheldon decided to retire from growing, reinforced by general conditions in the industry, where they were still making a living but barely enough to pay for replacing tractors and other equipment as they wore out.

The Sheldons retain half an acre of ground for themselves by their pleasant house on the edge of Draycott, the heart of the traditional strawberry-growing area. The rest is grassed down and let to their son-in-law, a local farmer. Now they grow just four rows of strawberries for themselves and their friends. At the peak in the early 1960s, their market-garden took up fifteen acres, one of the larger holdings in the area. But since growing demands a great deal of personal attention, when his father retired David Sheldon decided to reduce this to six acres. They have two daughters and five grandchildren living nearby, while Father died in early 1994, aged 91, long retired but still working on the holding and an important part of the workforce to the end.

I asked him how it all began.

"The original family came over from France or Belgium in the sixteenth century, when the Huguenots were driven out by the Catholics – I have been doing some research into this recently. They settled round Birmingham and were well-known tapestry-makers; in fact, one of the tapestries is in Warwick Castle. My branch eventually arrived in Cheddar in 1815. James Sheldon was a millwright who built six mills on the River Yeo, one of which remains in the yard of Scorse, the builders, with the Sheldon name on it. We are related to the Sheldon of Sheldon Jones, the Wells agricultural merchants, as well as many others in the area."

David Sheldon, strawberry grower.

"Your father started the business, how did you come into it?"

"My schooling covered the whole period of the war. I went to the Blue School in Wells, very different from nowadays, plenty of discipline and you were made to work. The staff wore gowns and you knew what you were there for. I took the train there and back each day, though there were occasions when it ran very late because of bombing elsewhere, so we missed some lessons. Then, on leaving school, I joined up with Dad and worked with him, taking over at his retirement in 1968."

"What crops did you grow?"

"When I started there was greater variety than now. The early nature of the slopes encouraged us to grow anything which suited the soil and the markets. Strawberries always have been important but another useful crop was anemones. They were a winter crop, but the trouble was that they poisoned the ground and we soon found they had to be rotated with a grass ley to restore the soil for the next crop. If you planted even an inch overlap between old and new ground the anemones would not grow. It was this problem that finally finished them off, though they grew well here and were profitable.

"There were other crops which did well for a while, then fell by the wayside as they became uneconomic for one reason or another. We grew an acre of broad-beans, another of runner beans, some spring cabbage and even early potatoes, excellent for cleaning the soil. Gradually all our markets were eroded by overseas suppliers coming in through newly opened-up air routes or improved cross-Channel services. In the last few years of our growing the real profit had gone; we made a living but only just, in spite of being one of the larger holdings."

"How did the strawberry market start here in the Cheddar valley?"

"It seems that it all really happened to any scale in 1890, when local growers grubbed out woods on the slopes above Shipham cross-roads and this continued along the valley through Axbridge, Cheddar, Draycott, Westbury and Rodney Stoke. They found virgin soil which suited strawberries well, with the south-facing slopes providing the perfect climate. Trains were able to despatch them in perfect condition virtually anywhere in the country. In those days it was possible to make an adequate living from as little as an acre of strawberries, right up to 1940 – but remember this was the time when you could survive on three cows for a self-sufficient life. One farmer over at Glastonbury made a good living from eight acres, six of cider apples and the rest supporting a few cows. This is unimaginable now."

"What happened then?"

"At this time there was no electricity, no television and people used oil lamps. They needed less in those days, going to bed when it was dark and rising early to work. Now we have to work to provide ourselves with television, outings, holidays and all the machines which go to make our lives easier. Each one of these means you need more crops to support you. The war changed everything and then, as affluence came, we needed to earn more to meet these expectations. At the same time competition from abroad cut prices.

"Of course the whole economy, before the war and immediately after, was built around the railways and the growers. I remember when the better-off, more established, growers took their crops by horse and cart to the station, while those who could not afford them pushed hand-carts. But it was an amazingly complex and efficient system, delivering strawberries in perfect condition all over the country by the small hours of the morning. Rail was kind to the fruit, the lorries that came after would shake and bruise the strawberries."

"You say it was a complex system, how many trains were there each day?"

"During the short three week period of the season there were four trains a day which distributed our fruit throughout Britain. The first left at 2pm, with strawberries from Draycott, Cheddar and Axbridge stations, delivering in Sunderland, Newcastle, Glasgow and Edinburgh. Another delivered to Manchester, Liverpool, Bradford and Accrington, while a third train served the Birmingham area. The final one left at ten in the evening for Bristol and Cardiff markets. The strawberries they carried were immaculate and arrived undamaged. When Beeching closed down the Strawberry Line in 1963, he inflicted great damage on the area and the strawberry industry. It was the beginning of our decline."

"But what about lorries? Couldn't they cope?"

"The system could not cope at that time. For a start the lorries were hard-sprung and damaged the fruit. Then there was no developed network ready to deliver to all the places where we had served the markets. We became remote from our markets and they died. We had to sell where we could get the transport or to people who made their own arrangements. Now most people rely on selling to the supermarket chains, though that has many problems because they concentrate on appearance rather than taste – our speciality. The multiples look for long shelf-life at the expense of everything else. Loads are rejected because of some small blemish or uneven colouring rather than looking for flavoursome fruit which are good to eat. Hard, bright red fruit are better for this than the softer strawberries we used to pride ourselves on producing. It's sad but a fact of life."

"What changes have you seen since you started?"

All the villages were devoted to the strawberry industry. Everything was geared up to that frantic three weeks of the year when money came in and bills could be paid. The local shops, particularly after Christmas, would give credit to local families until the seasonal cheques came in for strawberries or strawberry picking. The three weeks finished around 24th June, Mabbuts Tuesday as it was called locally, though I do not know where the name came from. This was the day when the later fruit from other parts of Britain flooded the market and the price dropped right back. We made our money and our reputation from the very early crops we were able to produce.

"In those days there were as many as fifteen reps staying locally, buying strawberries from the growers first thing in the morning, anxious to fill their needs. The price varied from day to day, according to weather and demand, and tempers got heated when the demand was not as much as growers thought, but the reps were a thick-skinned lot and came back even when they had been driven out the previous day. Baskets were made all the year round by the specialists, Scorse's, providing local employment, and the villages would be full of scurrying carts during those brief few weeks, for a great deal of fruit was despatched."

"How much?"

"Before the war the total crop, at just over a ton an acre, was around four hundred tons, giving a daily output of just under twenty tons. After the war that rose to five or more tons per acre with a daily output of around a hundred tons."

"That's a big increase."

"Yes, it all started in the war when we were encouraged to grow as much as we could and new virus-free stocks were introduced which raised crops considerably. Provided you used this new stock there were no restrictions on the amount of land that could be used for growing."

"Tell me, how were strawberries grown and what varieties?"

"It was frantic for the three weeks of the season's picking. We hired seventy people for our fifteen acres and sent buses round to bring them in to work. Now there is a great deal of self-picking to keep costs down.

"Like all crops grown intensively, strawberries suffer from a variety of ailments which either spoil the appearance or reduce the yield. Red core, viruses, wilts and eelworms are among the better known diseases or pests. One of our solutions was to rotate the ground, taking it out of production and putting it down to three year grass leys grazed by sheep and cattle. We had great success in sowing the grass with fifty per cent more seed than was recommended, to produce a rapid, thick sward which went on producing well over its life. The grass roots put fibre back into the soil and droppings add humus. More grass adds more droppings and leads to better crops later.

"Now strawberries are produced locally under cloches, they suit our crop better than tunnels, which are used elsewhere. The plants are kept for one year only and produce a pound of fruit to each plant. Cambridge Vigour is the finest variety for flavour and cropping, but lacks shelf-life, so is not grown as much as it should be."

"Apart from the trains, why else did you lose out in trade?"

"It was the coming of the Common Market in the 1970s, in combination with more frequent air services. We have always had competition from abroad, from the Po Valley in Italy, France and Belgium, but the fruit came by boat and suffered damage during their journeys. With air it arrived fresh and undamaged and could more than compete. Fruit came in from Kenya, California and Israel and worried growers for a few years but did not seem to affect us here as much as we had imagined. Then in 1979 things began to change for the worse, Italy no longer was a threat but was replaced by Spain."

"Why was that so much worse?"

"They went very thoroughly into the business of growing. Strawberries thrive near the sea, in good sun and in certain soils. The Spanish imported shiploads of soil into their coastal regions and found they had the perfect formula for growing very early strawberries cheaply, in walk-in tunnels. At the same time air-freight and even cross-channel vehicles were improving the whole time, making transport less of a problem and reducing damage to a minimum, though no-one seems to have asked the housewife whether she prefers cheapness and bright colours to the undoubted extra flavour of our berries.

"As a result of all this prices fell from just under £8 for 5lbs to £5 and finally to £3, at a time of inflation and growing costs. Between 1984 and '89 there was not sufficient margin for depreciation and replacement of essential equipment, such as tractors and cultivators. And the pressures on the strawberry business have continued ever since. Now there are less than a dozen growers left in the area, yet the soil and the climate remain as they always have, perfect for this crop."

"You mentioned the supermarkets and supplying direct."

"We were lucky. We supplied MacFisheries at Yate and found them very good to deal with, liking the product and all its qualities, looking for flavour as the main ingredient. Then they closed down in 1987 and we lost this market overnight. We had one of the big supermarket chains visit us but it became apparent that they were looking for something quite different to what we produced – absolute uniformity, hard fruit which would keep well, and colour – with no mention of taste. We decided to concentrate on selling locally and to those who were aware of our big advantage, top flavour."

"How did you manage in those difficult years?"

"We looked for new crops, different outlets, though we found few, and just plain worked hard. Father had found spring cabbage remunerative and this continued till the early 1980s when demand slackened with changes in eating habits. Then, from 1980 to 1987, we grew a great deal of lettuce, which spread the work over the winter. They were sown in November in peat blocks, planted out in February and cut in May; then along came

Iceberg, which took most of the market and was produced more economically overseas, once again cutting our market at a stroke."

"What is the main difference between now and when you started?"

"The work is not nearly so hard as it used to be. Now there are new and improved machines and black polythene which acts as a mulch to suppress the weeds, taking away much of the real back-breaking labour. For instance, it was very hard working behind a horse all day. Yes, it is an easier life now, so perhaps we should not grumble about some of the other changes for the worse, though it is becoming increasingly difficult to make a living in spite of the wonderful soil and climate."

We ended up wandering round his garden and admiring a most amazing collection of Delphiniums, some of which are new varieties which he raised himself and have attracted attention among the experts. The gradation of colours was quite exquisite, even on a grey and drizzly day. Clearly the skills of strawberry growing translate well to produce results in gardening. David Sheldon is not someone who sits back or lacks interests in his retirement from the demanding world of the professional strawberry-grower.

Brian Prewer, Caver

Talking to Brian and Brenda Prewer in their cottage at Priddy, it is not hard to imagine some of the five-mile network of Swildon's Hole which runs three hundred feet beneath them, and to understand their move to the village some six years ago, after over twenty-five in nearby Horrington. Brian came to Wells on finishing his RAF National Service and found work using his electronic skills with Thorn EMI at Wells. His interest in caving had begun while at the City of Bath Grammar School, where a group of sixth formers formed a small Club known as The Beechen Cliff Spaeleological Society. It was through caving friends that he met Brenda, who had been underground but decided it was not for her. However, having chosen to remain at home bringing up their daughter and two sons, she has been a vital member of the cave rescue team, acting as a co-ordinator on the radio telephone link.

After forty years in caving, Brian has a great deal of knowledge to share about Mendip underground. He lives very much within the caving ambience because Priddy is a village with a number of caving inhabitants. In fact, because the very popular Swildon's Hole can get somewhat congested at weekends, the 'locals' tend to visit it at any time within twenty-four hours during the middle of the week, with a thirty-year old tradition of Wednesdays being cave-digging night.

At the turn of the century the pioneer of Mendip caving, H. E. Balch, used to bicycle from Wells to his summer cottage in the hills. Nowadays, the members of the main clubs make use of their six stone-built hostels at Priddy, Oakhill, Nordrach and Green Ore. For roughly £2 per night, and £3 for visitors, club members have the use of showers, dormitories, cooking facilities and even libraries. Each hostel is the headquarters of one of the clubs, the better known of which include Mendip Nature Research Committee (originally formed by Balch); Wessex Cave Club; Bristol Exploration Club; Shepton Mallet Caving Club; the London-based Mendip Caving Group and the University of Bristol Spaeleological Society, some of whose members were the first to discover the famous GB Cavern at Charterhouse. Universities have contributed a great deal to caving, both through their students and in research. The other seventy or so Clubs which come to Mendip vary in size from twenty to a hundred members. They provide some facilities, such as equipment, but do not have their own headquarters, perhaps basing their activities from a pub or even someone's house.

Brian Prewer at Swildon's Hole entrance.

For relaxation, the Hunters Lodge Inn has been the local apres-cave for the dedicated for over sixty years, with a very involved landlord, Roger Dors, who is the third generation of his family to live there. His famous relative, Diana, was known to arrive in a white Rolls Royce for her Sunday lunch.

The Queen Victoria and the New Inn are also used by cavers, but to a lesser extent, being occupied mainly by weekend casuals seeking bed and breakfast.

Brian pointed out that in nearly all cases caves are on private land, so good relations must exist between cavers and owners, who are almost universally tolerant. Usually, there is a goodwill charge and sometimes the use of changing facilities, such as a nearby barn. Clubs keep keys to the caves, but generally there is no restriction for bona fide cavers.

While cavers try not to become involved in controversy over planning matters, sometimes they walk a tightrope between remaining on good terms with landowners and preserving a unique part of our heritage which, once destroyed, can never be replaced. There is also a fine line to be drawn between the need for stone and the local employment provided by quarries, as opposed to caving interests.

So, what about the thorny question of caves versus the increasing inroads of the quarrying companies? For instance, this has been a problem in Fairy Cave Quarry on East Mendip. Over the last forty years, the quarry has unearthed about sixteen caves there, containing some of the finest stalactite formations in Britain. One cave has been destroyed but the others were saved through using injunctions where water courses were in evidence. "It would seem the Court's view is that water is important, but caves are not," Brian commented. In situations like this, the National Caving Association deals at high level with Government Departments while Regional Councils operate locally.

Brian told us about Waterlip Quarry at Cranmore which came to an abrupt demise in the 1940's when an underground water course was broken into, flooding the whole area to a depth of fifty feet. Much the same happened at Vobster Quarry, resulting in a lake one-hundred-and-ten feet deep. Of course, this can only emphasise how detrimental to caves and water courses such quarrying can be, altering the whole aspect of water flow underground.

While on the subject of water, Brian pointed out that it is only because of caving activities that the complex hydrology of Mendip has been studied and understood. Tests used to be made by putting dyes in the water but more sophisticated techniques now involve *Lycopodium* spores (of Club Moss), which are basically indestructible and can be detected in minute quantities. It is fascinating to hear that there is an 11-24 hour transit time of water through the five-mile network of tunnels from the entrance of Swildon's to its resurgence at Wookey Hole, and that this water is never more than eight-hundred feet below ground. In flood conditions water can travel from St Cuthberts Swallet, Priddy, to Wookey Hole in only eight hours. At one time it was assumed that all the water which vanished below ground on the Mendips would reappear at either Wookey Hole or Cheddar, but it is now known that water in the Burrington area goes to Rickford and Blagdon Lake. And can it really be true that, because of the depth it has to travel, Mendip water takes ten thousand years to reach Bath hot springs?

Having seen pictures of H.E. Balch and friends preparing to go underground in tweed suits, plus-fours and leather boots, we were interested to learn what the modern caver wears.

"Yes," said Brian, "wet suits are very useful in caves where water runs habitually, especially for divers, but the modern kit is now so good that cavers can keep pretty dry and warm in specially designed clothes made with a waterproof membrane. As for feet, we still cannot really improve on the vibram, commando-soled boot with a metal toe cap. There is now a Wellington boot available, with a similarly deep-grooved sole, which is also good, but trainers are not suitable. Teenagers wearing these have had accidents and they should never be worn when venturing underground."

"And what about light? How effective is a torch beam wavering round a huge cavern?"

"Well, of course, originally it was candles and how the early cavers managed I just cannot think. There must have been problems with flames blowing sideways or even out, and the limitations of depth of light. In fact, on special anniversaries, cavers have used candles and this has really brought home the difficulties. It actually took Balch something like six hours to cover the early stages of Swildon's, which today we can get through in about a quarter of an hour."

Cavers then experimented with the carbide lamps used by miners at such local collieries as Radstock. These were, and still are, very good as they give an even distribution of light and last indefinitely when spare stocks of carbide are mixed with water. This makes them excellent on trips lasting longer than the eight to ten hours' duration of the miners' rechargeable safety lights which are used nowadays on ordinary caving trips.

Of course, we had to ask the obvious. "Surely caving is a dangerous sport?"

Brian must have answered this many times before. "Far less than you might expect; you are about eight hundred times more likely to get injured playing football than down a cave!   On average, we have about eight to ten rescues a year, ranging from the trivial to the more serious, of which there might be two or three."

As a member of the Mendip Cave Rescue Organization (MRO), he filled us in on its history.   The second oldest organisation in the country after Yorkshire, it was founded in 1936 by Dr. Crook with members of the Wessex Cave Club and the University of Bristol Spaeleological Society.   Since then they have carried out approximately 350 rescues, which works out at just over six a year.   And that includes dogs, or even sheep, trapped in inaccessible spots.

The MRO acts as an agent for the Police, who contact them following a 999 call to the Taunton Control Room.   The cavers are the experts who take over, operating under the authority, and covered by the insurance, of the Police.   All MRO members are volunteers, entirely funded by donations from Clubs, individuals and fundraising functions.

With his wide experience, local caving knowledge and availability, Brian must be an obvious choice as a team member.   Historically, they have no constitution as such. There is a Secretary and Treasurer, and a group of twenty or so rescue wardens, whose number is self-perpetuating as they get to know who is reliable and of the right calibre to join them. There are about six wardens who between them, and with the help of their wives, are available for contact day and night.   The first call out should come to Brian and, while he prepares and sets off, Brenda goes into action on the telephone, calling up more volunteers, and keeping in touch with the rescuers.

Brian gave us an example of the time limits involved.   "Say the cavers enter the cave at 8.00am and the accident occurs two hours later.   You then have to allow at least an hour for someone to return to the surface and raise the alarm, so the very earliest the rescuers can get to the cave would be 11.30am.   Then about another hour to reach the injured person and, depending on conditions, anything up to five hours to get them out.   And this time could be doubled if the accident occurs deep underground."

"Are they carried, and just how do you manage round the narrow parts?"

"With difficulty.   Yes, we do carry and it's a slow job.   Quite often we need to replace tired rescuers.   That's where Brenda is so useful.   She starts by calling in local volunteers who can get there quickly, then rings those who live further away.   When they arrive they can take over from the first lot.

Good communication is vital.   We use a radio network to get food, etc., to the entrance as rescuers need looking after, too.   Lancaster University have developed a unique radio system operating through rock, which previously was not possible, and this hooks into the surface system to relay when we need the ambulance or medical help. The whole rescue costs the public surprisingly little, only the police car and the ambulance. Cavers rescue cavers, and it's quite likely that a local caving doctor will come and help. Heaven forbid that we should need so many, but it is possible for us to get up to three hundred cavers to a site within an hour, all stemming from the organising wardens."

We had a look at their Club Magazine which, among lots of interesting articles, gives descriptions of the handling of an accident. It all helps for future call outs. And, of course, Clubs run their own first aid courses.

"What's the main cause of accidents, would you say?"

"They're usually known as the 3 Fs. Falls (probably the most frequent cause), followed by flood and then failure of equipment, perhaps when lights give out or a party gets itself lost."

Brian said that the worst problems are caused by cavers who either leave no message of their intended route, or something so vague that it is equally unhelpful. He remembered a particularly stressful rescue a few years ago, involving two Cadets who left a message saying they were going caving somewhere on the Mendips. When they did not return to Sandhurst after the weekend a massive rescue operation was set in motion. In two days seventy per cent of the four hundred caves in the area were searched, which is a formidable task by any estimation and must have involved many volunteers. They would have carried on with the last thirty per cent but then heard that the young men had been located in the Channel Isles, having deliberately laid a false trail.

Pondering on this thoughtlessness, we could not help wondering if there were any other problems that caused particular worries?

"Oh yes – and this is something relatively new. When I first started caving there were no 'professional' leaders. Anyone who was sufficiently interested joined a Club and could then go down with a group of experienced cavers. If anything went wrong or they could not cope, there was always someone to help or give advice. But today we have Activity Centres which offer packages of weekend courses, including caving. A leader takes down quite large parties of novices, half of whom probably aren't there for the caving at all, and that's when problems can occur. It is very difficult to keep control of a large party of novices. Even schools are starting to do this. I feel very concerned that these Centres are destroying the fabric of what Club caving is all about. Traditionally, cavers have been enthusiasts with a long-term interest in the sport. They approach it cautiously and learn gradually. These Centres offer a quick experience and then move on to something else, which could be a recipe for disaster."

In spite of such worries, Brian obviously continues to gain immense interest and satisfaction from his caving, and not least is the variety of people who are attracted to it. He has a wide circle of friends, and could no doubt call up instant, personal help from a plumber, solicitor or doctor, to name but a few. Brenda nodded agreement at this, "Yes, we have some very good social gatherings with people of many interests, once you get them off the subject of caving, of course. It costs very little to join a Club – about £20 a year."

Reinforced in our view that, sadly, we come from species *claustrophobicus*, out came the cliché. What makes these apparently ordinary, sane people vanish underground?

"There are several aspects to it," Brian replied patiently. "It is adventurous while not being competitive. Some people like to study geology, others are interested in hydrology and cave hydrography. There is also the fascination of the special biology of creatures that live in total darkness or just a glimmer of light. Some cavers use their skills in photography or surveying. We spend a lot of time in digging out caves and looking for new routes. When you think that we are removing glacial debris from the last Ice Age, which was about ten thousand years ago, you can imagine how compelling it is to attempt to get back to the original."

And since one good cliché deserves another, he added, "And, of course, because they're there."

The final question was, could we take a photograph?

Brian thought for a moment, then said, "Would you like to see the entrance to Swildon's?"

Would we just. Since studying the subject, this has become a hopeful ambition, just so long as it really is only the entrance. So we went out into the bright sunshine of a typically windy June morning on Mendip and crossed the fields. Dropping down to a little copse with a wide, shallow stream, we saw a circular stone shelter with an open steel door. Standing by a triangular hole in the floor, the water ran fast and quite full beneath our feet, vanishing into a rocky black hole that appeared to drop away steeply. And cavers really travel miles to spend their weekends in situations such as this? Yes, after talking to Brian, it is possible to understand the attraction and pull of this mysterious world. Would that we were brave enough to go, too.

John Boyd, Conservationist

An active, upright figure, always peering at something by his feet or in the sky above, John has long retired from his partnership in a firm of solicitors, but acts like a man of considerably less years, keeping up with the youngest during long days out in the field. His lifetime experience of the landscape, people and wildlife of Somerset makes a conversation with him of particular interest.

Brought up in Leigh Woods on the far side of Clifton Suspension Bridge, he could walk out of the door and into unspoiled, extensive and empty woodlands full of all sorts of wildlife and flowers. Red squirrels played in their garden and there were glades in the woods full of butterflies and flowers.

Ever since, he has been involved in watching wildlife, searching out its behaviour and photographing it. Photography began with Box Brownies and plate cameras aimed at birds, before moving to his present love – insects, but now using modern equipment which enables him to focus on the smallest creature and produce brilliant slides which are shown to many appreciative audiences in the area.

John Boyd can always find something of interest.

The family lived in Bristol to be near the office, but in 1972 moved to Draycott, where they have lived ever since. His wife Clé shares many of his interests and is currently running a survey of otters in Somerset.

First memories of Mendip were in the mid-1920s when his family used to drive out to Mendip Mines at Charterhouse for weekend picnics. Waldegrave Pool was then, as now, one of the honeypots attracting crowds of people, while Charterhouse was wild and empty, as it still is. Between the mid-1930's and 1979 he visited Mendip infrequently, spending most of his limited free time on the Levels round Wedmore. In those days most people worked on Saturdays, which did not leave much spare time.

However, John became heavily involved with Mendip again in 1979 when he was appointed a warden for the newly promoted 'project area'. In that year, for the first time, the Countryside Commission funded a Project Area Officer for Cheddar Gorge and Blackdown, under the auspices of the Somerset Trust. Bill Butcher in turn recruited a number of voluntary wardens to help him, John being amongst this number. Their job was manifold, in one very dry period they were asked to firewatch over a huge area; otherwise they were there to offer help to the public in understanding the project, the countryside and its wildlife, as well as keeping an eye out for vandals and trouble-makers. They were really public relations officers, having to use tact as well as knowledge. The scheme was supposed to be handed over to the Local Authority after three years but in the end extended to five.

This period served to initiate John into the detail and fabric of this fascinating countryside and concentrated his interests. While his later surveys continued to take in parts of the Levels, the main thrust of his interest is now firmly in Mendip.

In 1980 he became Reserve Manager of Black Rock for the Somerset Trust. This proved fascinating. On his first day he and his wife were walking in broad daylight and came across a family of badgers, with the cubs playing out in the open, unworried by their presence. The extended family appeared to consist of thirteen individuals and set the scene for their enjoyment of this reserve.

In 1982 he changed to become Reserve Manager for Priddy Mineries, with its pools and gruffy ground, which he retains to this day and which, I suspect, is his favourite spot on Mendip. He has no doubt that without the Somerset Trust's management of reserves such as this, and their influence on other landowners, a great deal of wildlife would have been lost, though not everything is achieved instantly.

Waldegrave Pool was originally made to wash ore being mined nearby. This part of Mendip has an impermeable podsol on a base of Old Red

Sandstone so the pool was constructed at a low point, where rain would run in from the surrounding hill slopes. This worked perfectly as originally designed, but is no longer so effective, with deep ploughing on surrounding slopes breaking the pan, affecting drainage and fertility.

Heather is disappearing quite fast and noticeably. One year a large clump held thirteen Emperor moth caterpillars, the next year there was no trace of the clump. Heather will live up to fifty years in normal circumstances, becoming leggier and larger. If burnt or cut every ten years it should renew itself from the base. John has been experimenting with clearing patches and sowing seed. This is successful but very labour intensive, while experiments with cutting and burning have not yielded much success to date, because the heather was too old. Stripping turf and sowing should keep heather going and give reasonable stands in the long term. If not, the insect and plant life of the reserve will alter.

They have been more successful with controlling the water-level in the pool, though that, too, has had its moments. In theory, the level is controlled by a hatch at one end, the water being taken in during winter rains, then gradually evaporating in summer. The hatch was originally wooden, but a spate of vandalism forced a change to concrete. Then the pool started leaking at the dam but this has been strengthened and all appears well. The end result is that the pool has a 'normal' level of nearly a foot higher than previously and provides near-perfect conditions for the many dragonflies for which it is famous. It all goes to show that looking after a reserve requires a great deal of attention to detail.

"What changes have you noticed in the appearance of Mendip?"

"By 1979 most of the the changes caused by the revolution in farming practice had already taken place. Changes since then have been minimal, with some ploughing of old pasture and further deterioration of unrepaired stone walls."

He paused a moment to think. "Although probably the most obvious change has been the introduction of large-scale free-range pig keeping on some of the top fields. In one instance this has been used as a means of clearing a field for ploughing and grain crops. But whatever happens later, it makes a tremendous mess and destroys forever the old pasture-land on which they live."

Of course change is something which happens continually in farming and has led to the diversity of landscape which is so much a part of England. Apart from the seemingly inevitable loss of some old unspoiled pastures and the flowers and plants which go with them, John is not generally worried about the future of Mendip, although a question-mark lies over the business of quarrying. It appears that quarries are going deeper now they are reaching the boundaries of the areas for which they have planning permission.

"Is this affecting the water-table and will it bring long-term problems?"

"There is much talk about this, with some saying that the present levels of quarrying are having an effect on the flow of water as far away as the Pump Room at Bath, and there are worries about the Mendips still being able to supply the greater part of the water to Bristol Waterworks. Deep quarrying could destroy the aquifer, with disastrous results. However, I believe that if no extensions are allowed then the position should be all right. My real worry lies in what happens as present quarries come to the end of their life. Will their boundaries be extended?"

Of particular concern to John are the woodlands of Mendip, features that are very much a part of the landscape and sources of considerable invertebrate life and flora. Much of the wildlife in woods cannot move far and so does not readily colonise new sites. The most valuable woods are therefore 'ancient' ones, those that have been established for hundreds of years.

"There are two types of ancient woodland, of which the commonest is 'coppice', where a different section was cut to the ground each year to provide firewood (which was the main heating fuel) and all the small timber required for repairs and other uses. Local conditions determine the speed at which timber regenerates and therefore the length of time that the complete rotation took, probably between ten and twenty years. Thus, there was always a variety of plots, from newly cleared (with a profusion of woodland flowers) to ready to cut again, giving a complete range of habitats to suit the plants and animals in the wood.

"The other type, 'wild wood', received no management ever, trees being left to grow to maturity, fall and decay, making a glade and providing dead and decaying wood as a habitat for invertebrates. These woods were not economical in any sense and therefore unusual. Coppice created a profusion of plants and animals, but of limited species, while wild wood produced more species, some of them very rare now, as they may be wingless or confined by their life-cycle to a short distance from their birth point. The last planned coppicing was stopped in the 1920s, when the need for firewood and stakes diminished and it was no longer economic to manage the woods in this way."

"But surely some coppicing has been done since?"

"Yes, but only as a part of the move to conservation and then only tentatively and experimentally. The real problem is the gap since the 20s."

"Why? Can't you just start up again?"

"It's not as simple as that, for many of the woods are smaller than they were. For successful coppicing you need to cut a patch every year, but it should be of reasonable size to provide the right habitat succession for all types of insects. A coppiced tree can be virtually everlasting. It renews itself and some of the really old ones, in Cheddar Wood for instance, may be fourteen feet or more across, with a hollow centre where the original trunk was.

Another factor is that, since coppicing stopped, some woodland has been cleared for agriculture, while most of those left are the awkward ones which are not easily accessible. Although there is now a market for firewood, the cost of cutting and removal still makes it an uneconomic proposition."

"So what is the answer?" I asked.

"I'm not sure," John reflected, "The management of each wood has to be decided according to its particular circumstances. Unfortunately, woods are fragmented and far apart and it is unlikely that there will be much movement of species between them. Therefore one should continue the previous form of management, whatever it was, and hope that after this lapse of time there will be sufficient of the species left, although it might be possible to change a coppice to a wild wood, which maintains diversity naturally. I believe we might manage an old, neglected coppiced wood to produce the same effect, but it would be a very long term project, going beyond existing lifetimes. You would cut trees in plots every few years, clearing space for natural re-growth, but leaving the trees to rot in place on the ground, encouraging insect species. Gradually this would have the effect of spreading the age of the various parts of the wood, and eventually it could be allowed to revert to its own natural cycle."

"Is there anywhere round Mendip you could see this happening?"

"Yes, Cheddar Wood, with its unique small-leaved lime population. It is large enough and well-suited to this method."

"Why are these woods so important?"

"They have been a feature of Mendip since time immemorial and they contain a quite different variety of fauna and flora to the open grasslands or the stone walls, which are another important habitat. And, of course, a great many people walk the woods and learn about wildlife from them."

"May we move on now to the weekly surveys of flora and invertebrates which you carry out with your helpers. What do they do?"

"I carry them out on behalf of the Somerset Wildlife Trust and most are on their reserves, though we may be asked to look at other places of special interest. The reasons for the survey may be several: checking for plants or creatures which need protection; listing species to determine ways of

Waldegrave Pool, the heart of Mendip dragonfly surveys.

managing a reserve initially; or monitoring change after a period of management."

"How long have you been doing this?"

"The invertebrate survey began in 1990, with the intention of teaching people about dragonflies, but developed into a regular survey carried out every Saturday of the year, weather allowing, covering the whole invertebrate world. This information is fed periodically into the Somerset Records Centre and is used in determining management strategy or the viability of an area for reserve status.

"The botanical surveys were first started eleven years ago, in a deliberate effort to get to know more about the Mendip reserves, and have proved invaluable. They take place every Tuesday throughout the year and, in addition to providing information, have served to train people to carry out this important work elsewhere".

"Why is it so important?"

"It is vital to know what is happening to populations of wildlife and flora, to see whether they are declining or increasing. Continual

159

monitoring is the only way to discover what effects present management methods are having. For instance, we have found out that some management practices carried out on reserves, with the very best of intentions, have actually sped up the decline of certain vulnerable species such as the large blue butterfly.

"So little is known about invertebrates, in particular, that it is a matter of extending the bounds of knowledge. Many people watch birds, few are so knowledgeable about insects."

"So, more knowledge is vital?"

"Yes, we know little about the smaller, less visible, creatures and tend to manage reserves for birds and other high-profile animals, though there are signs that this attitude is changing as we find out more."

"You feel strongly about this."

"I do. I think we are too namby-pamby in our reserve management at times, worrying about appearance rather than what suits the creatures best, although there is an element of ignorance behind it. It is this ignorance we are trying to address by way of these surveys."

8 Enjoying Mendip

There are many ways of appreciating Mendip, but it is principally an outside place, wild and beautiful, to be enjoyed by those exploring its countryside and the world beneath.

The delights of Cheddar Gorge, with its shops, conducted tours of caves, Jacob's Ladder ascent to the heights of the cliffs and other communal activities are too well known to warrant comment here. Tens of thousands visit each year, to gaze up at the splendour of the Gorge and look round the concentration of attractions below. Many do not realise that there is a wilder, empty part above, well worth exploring, some of it with activities to make their visits enjoyable, others offering that empty peace which needs no facilities.

This chapter concentrates on this wilder part, the empty places where the air is fresh, the grass truly green and skies vast. This is what the great bulk of Mendip is all about – on a par with, though differing in character from, the other great wild places and walking areas of England – Exmoor, Dartmoor, the Peak District, the Yorkshire Dales and the Lake District.

What are the outdoor activities for which people visit the Mendip Hills?

Walking

For the great majority, Mendip represents an ideal place for walking, with magnificent views, particularly to the south over the Somerset Levels a thousand feet below, stretching across to the church tower on Glastonbury Tor and far beyond on a clear day. Or looking across Bridgwater Bay and the Bristol Channel to the Black Mountains and Brecon Beacons in Wales and the blue heights of Dunkery on Exmoor.

The top ranges from wide open walks across limestone sheep-sward to narrow sunken lanes hidden in steep hedges; from parts where it is possible to look across twenty miles of open countryside to places that feel as if the bounds of hearing are the limits of the world, where the sounds of wrens and other small birds fill the consciousness.

Mendip is not a place of formal walks, there are so many it could be possible to explore them over a lifetime; look at any Ordnance Survey map and the public footpaths are everywhere, like spider's webs on the paper. For long Mendip has been one of the lesser-known areas, but recently this has been remedied by the publication of two new Explorer maps from the Ordnance Survey. Sheet 4, Mendip Hills West, and Sheet 5, Mendip Hills East, cover a much larger area than just the hills. At 2.5 inches to the mile, they provide every detail of the land, ranging from Winscombe in the west to Frome in the east and from Blagdon in the north down to Castle Cary, covering the eastern part of the Levels also.

It would be impossible to mention other than one or two walks here, but there are some excellent books available, including one from Ex Libris Press, *Mendip Rambles*, by Peter Wright, which offers a selection of twelve walks covering the area.

However, there is one 'official' walk through some remarkable countryside. The West Mendip Way was put together by various Rotary Clubs in honour of the Queen's Silver Jubilee. It is around thirty miles long and has been built up by waymarking and linking a network of public footpaths, bridleways and roads to provide a route from Uphill, near Weston-super-Mare, across the top of Mendip to Wells.

The route is marked with posts with the name cut into them and discs showing the direction. As with many such routes, all is not necessarily clear. Barbed wire appears at times, crops bar the way and gates may be wired shut, but the numbers of people using the route are rising and these problems lessen as time goes on.

The route is complicated and a guide-book is helpful – try *West Mendip Way*, by Derek Moyes – but is well worth the effort, even if carried out in stages over several weeks.

Briefly, the route goes from Uphill to Bleadon, then Loxton, a pretty little place just short of the M5. From there the way wanders along the edge of the hill, past the Webbington Country Club, uphill beside Crook Peak, then by Compton Bishop through King's Wood to Shipham. From this ancient mining village the path leads along the valley to the riding centre at Tyning's Farm. From there the route diverts from the main Charterhouse road, making its way south, eventually through ancient Long Wood and past the spectacular cliff of Black Rock to the upper reaches of Cheddar Gorge.

Crossing the road and ascending through the woods clothing Cheddar north cliffs, walkers emerge to find some spectacular views, especially if a short diversion is taken to the north towards the mouth of the Gorge to look down on Cheddar Reservoir, with all the Levels and the Severn Sea spread out in front.

But the Mendip Way goes in the opposite direction, along the southern slopes of Mendip, through delectable Maskell's Wood, by way of Bradley Cross, beside former and still working strawberry fields, eventually reaching Draycott, a pleasant stone village. No sooner down into the village than the route ascends once more, though allowing a good look at the village.

A short three miles beyond Draycott, the way enters ancient Priddy, unofficial capital of Mendip top, past the stack of hurdles on the green and on into Dursdon Drove, heading downhill. Next stop is Ebbor Gorge, an exhausting climb in and out, emerging onto the road to Wookey Hole. Still descending, Wells finally comes in sight.

No-one would take the West Mendip Way if they wanted to get from A to B, it twists and wanders like a meandering stream, but there are few finer ways of seeing this spectacular slice of Mendip

While there are many other worthwhile walks, these are just a few which we enjoy particularly: Black Down, entered from a path up beside Tyning's Farm; the mouth of Cheddar Gorge, by way of the north cliff path mentioned in the Mendip Way above; and the walk along Draycott Sleights, the Somerset Trust reserve above Draycott. All these have that particular extra magic which makes their memory special.

Most of Mendip meets at Priddy Sheep Fair every August.

Riding

For riding enthusiasts there must be few more spectacular and enjoyable places than Mendip in which to enjoy the sport. Others do not always take such a charitable view, claiming that the continual passage of horses on narrow paths soon reduces them to a quagmire and then a rocky scar. This has led to some difficult moments in enquiries into opening up more bridle paths, with the argument becoming even more heated with the coming of the 4-wheel drive vehicle driven along such paths as a sport.

However it is viewed, Mendip is a paradise for riders and a great many people use it in this manner. It is possible to learn to ride, take long treks and see much of the top without actually owning or keeping a horse of your own, for there are well-equipped riding centres catering for all needs.

The whole area round Shipham, Rowberrow, Black Down and Beacon Batch is rich in bridleways, leading right up to the northern scarp face. However, most of the rest of Mendip, east and west, is remarkably bare of such tracks, according to the latest maps. Both Tynings Riding School, between Shipham and Charterhouse, and the Shipham Equestrian Centre feed into this network of bridleways.

Gliding

This sport is well-established on Mendip now, through the club set high up above Draycott. This is a direct descendant of the first efforts at gliding in the area by the Air Training Corps, just after the War, when advanced courses were held from a field above Draycott Sleights. It turned out to be ideal for gaining the height needed to provide good flights, as well as being blessed with plenty of thermals in the right weather.

Nowadays the sight of gliders circling high above western Mendip is an accepted part of the scenery and many must wonder how it feels to look down on the whale-hump of Mendip, the sea at Weston-super-Mare and beyond to Wales. There is no need just to wonder. The Mendip Gliding Club offers trial flights to those who wish to experience this particular brand of magic, soaring up, yet powered only by the engineless aerodynamics of the graceful glider.

Seven years ago the Club took over from the RAF at this site. In 1994 it had nearly ninety members and owns two single-seater and two two-seater gliders available for the use of members. The whole organisation is voluntary, depending on members for everything that takes place – the winch which launches the gliders into the air, duty instructors and help with pushing gliders out for launching, as well as recovery at the end of a flight. Charges are based on the cost of a launch plus so much a minute while the glider is in the air. A launch fee is charged for those bringing their own glider.

Gliding takes place at weekends and on Thursdays, and all are welcome. We cannot think of a finer way of viewing this marvellous part of the world.

Caving

The previous chapter gave a detailed insight into this sport, as seen by one who has participated all his life. Suffice it to say that this is perhaps the sport for which the area is best known. Any weekend visitor to the area cannot miss parties of cavers piling into or out of their minibuses or cars, helmeted, booted and slung about with ropes and other equipment, while local pubs are full of cavers discussing their adventures of the past day or planning the next expedition.

As Brian Prewer remarked, the best way into the sport is through one of the long-established clubs which take beginners in hand, introducing them properly to the joys and wonder of the sport, as part of a team of experienced cavers.

The area is riddled with caves and there are many books on the subject, as well as a shop in Wells, Bat Products, which devotes itself mainly to equipping cavers with gear and reading matter. Caving has the reputation of being a friendly sport but the first step is to find out whether you are one of those who enjoy going underground. Mendip is the place to find this out, and if not caving, then walking, riding or gliding are all there for the asking.

Places of Special Interest

Museums

King John's Hunting Lodge Museum
The Square, Axbridge. Local history, geology, archaeology, ceramics and glass. Tel: 01934-732012.

East Somerset Railway
Steam-train museum. Open March-December, but days vary. East Cranmore, Tel: 01749-880417.

Gough's Cave Museum
Cheddar, all year round. Relics of ancient man's life in the caves. Tel: 01934-742343.

Wells Museum
Cathedral Green, Wells. Open all year, but days vary. Early Iron Age items from Wookey Hole, folk relics and the geology and life of the region. Varied and fascinating. There is a library attached with many archives from the area.
Tel: 01749-673477.

Wookey Hole Museum
Small but interesting, with many relics found in the caves from Iron Age, Roman days and later. Summer and winter. Also Titania's Palace, one of the most important and largest collection of miniature items in the world. Summer only. Tel: 01749-672243.

Churches, Cathedrals and Closes

Bishop's Palace, Wells.
Palace and Grounds open April-October, Wednesday, Thursday and Sunday afternoons. Every day in August and Bank Holiday Mondays. Tel: 01749-674483.

St. Peter & St. Paul
Shepton Mallet, open daily.

Vicar's Close
Wells, the public can walk here at any time.

Wells Cathedral
Every day until dark, except during services. Tel: 01749-674483.

General

Burrington Combe
Free parking and walking.

Cheddar Gorge and Village
Park and pay in Gorge. The various attractions, Caves and Jacob's Ladder, the Cheese village and other exhibitions are by individual arrangement. General, Tel: 01934-744071. Caves, Tel: 01934-742343.

East Somerset Railway
Steam rides on the Strawberry Line.
March-December, but days vary. Museum, see above. East Cranmore, Tel:
01749-880417.

Ebbor Gorge
National Trust. Free Parking and
walking. Circular route through spectacular gorge, which is also a wildlife
reserve with unusual plants and insects. Information leaflets for sale in
car-park.

King John's Hunting Lodge
Axbridge, Tel: 01934-732012.

Mendip Gliding Club
Gliding, for learners and the experi-
enced, above Draycott.
Tel: 01749-870312.

Nunney Castle
Free entry at any time.

Priddy Sheep Fair
Held in August each year.

Draycott Strawberry Fair
Held in June each year.

Axbridge Blackberry Fair
Held in September each year.
Shipham Equestrian Centre
Horse-riding and trekking, Shipham,
Tel: 01934-843522.

Tynings Riding School
Horse-riding and trekking, Charterhouse, Tel: 01934-742501.

Wookey Hole Caves and Exhibitions
Paper-making by hand, caves, Witch
of Wookey, fairground machinery.
Tel: 01749-672243.

Tourist Information Centres

Cheddar, the Gorge.
Tel: 01934-744071.

Wells, Town Hall, Market Place.
Tel: 01749-672552

Some Special Walks

West Mendip Way
Runs thirty miles, from Uphill, near
Weston-super-Mare, to Wells, entering
our part of Mendip at Crook Peak.
From there by way of Shipham, Cheddar Cliffs, Priddy and Wookey Hole,
to Wells, taking in some of the finest
of the limestone scenery. For details
see *West Mendip Way, the Walkers
Guide*, by Derek Moyes, Mendip Publishing.

Crook Peak and Wavering Down
Starts at ST 386565, below Crook Peak.
Part of the West Mendip Way but spe-
cial in its own right.

See *Mendip Rambles, 12 Walks Around
the Mendip Hills*, by Peter Wright, Ex
Libris Press.

Further Reading

Many books have been written about its hills and people and the following bibliography is by no means exhaustive; representing only those we have consulted in the course of our research.

Wells and other libraries hold a mass of local information, original papers from the past, archaeological society minutes and pamphlets, as well as excellent packs made up for each parish in the area. These are well worth consulting, containing photocopies of relevant information on population and special events, taken from the original source.

Finally we would mention that the serious original researcher ought to visit the reference library at Wells Museum. Its hours of opening vary and a telephone call to the Museum is recommended before visiting. Tel: 01749-673477. A great many old books, documents and sources are kept there and a morning browsing through these is never wasted.

A History of Somerset, Robert Dunning (Phillimore, 1983).

A History of Somerset, Robert Dunning (Somerset County Library, 1987).

A Portrait of Somerset, Bryan Little (Robert Hale, 1971).

Book of Somerset Villages, Sheila Bird (Dovecote Press, 1986).

The Somerset Village Book, (Somerset Federation of Women's Institutes, 1988).

Old Somerset Fairs, Muriel Walker.

Domesday Studies, Rev. R W Eyton (Reeves & Turner, 1880).

Wessex from AD1000, J H Bettey (Longman, 1986).

The Mendip Hills, Shirley Toulson (Victor Gollancz, 1984).

Man & The Mendips, (The Mendip Society, 1971).

Mendip Country, Jillian Powell & Julia Davey (Bossiney Books, 1987).

The Mendips, Coysh, Mason & Waite (Robert Hale & Co, 1971).

Old Mendip, Robin Atthill (Bran's Head Books, 1984).

The Mendips in Old Photographs, Chris Howell (Alan Sutton, 1990).

The Seaboard of Mendip, Francis A Knight (Alis Press, 1988).

Some Buildings of Mendip, R D Reid (The Mendip Society, 1979).

West Mendip Way, Derek Moyes (Mendip Publishing, 1987).

Geological Highlights of the West Country, W Macfadyen (Butterworths, 1970).

Mendip Underground, A Caver's Guide, David Irwin & Antony Knibbs (Castle Carey Press).

The History of Mendip Caving, Peter Johnson (David & Charles, 1967).

The Mines of Mendip, J W Gough (David & Charles, 1967).

The Dorset & Somerset Canal, Kenneth R Clew (David & Charles, 1971).

The Somerset & Dorset Railway, Robin Atthill (David & Charles, 1985).

About the Authors

Some three decades ago, Robin and Romey Williams lived with their three daughters on almost the highest point on Mendip, in an isolated house looking out on stone walls and fields. The place has changed little since then but now they look up at Mendip from their house on the Levels. They still spend much time walking and exploring the uplands, especially at weekends as members of the Mendip Invertebrate Group, which is gradually surveying much of the area to see the effects of change on the insect population.

Robin was born in Africa but moved back to England when a few weeks old. He has been here ever since, except for some time in the Far and Middle East on assignment as a management consultant. Now he is retired and able to devote more time to exploring Somerset, its wildlife and landscape. He has written about, and photographed, Mendip and the Levels for many years. In such magazines as *Country Life*, *The Field* and *Environment Now*. He runs his own photographic library covering Somerset scenery and British wildlife, with special emphasis on insects.

Romey is a native of Somerset and has lived in the country almost all her life, although during that time Weston-super-Mare has transferred from Somerset to Avon and now back again. Brock, her dog, keeps her in close touch with the countryside and she has a number of local interests which keep her busy. She writes short stories and articles in her spare time.

With the exception of a year away in Oxford the family has spent its whole life in Somerset and has an abiding curiosity about the county, its history and future. Robin and Romey are authors of *The Somerset Levels*, another book in this series, while Robin has written a book about the history and wildlife of Tealham Moor.

INDEX

Note: Main references are in bold type; illustrations are referred to in italic. Some items are listed under a group heading, viz. caves, monarchs, pubs, rivers, roads

Greyhound Inn 76
Hunters Lodge **26**, 149
King's Arms 91
Knatchbull Arms 98
Mendip Inn **26**
Miners Arms **26**, 43, 94, 97, 122
New Inn 146
Old Down Inn **26**, 84
Ploughboy Inn **27**, 85
Slab House **27**
Swan Inn 96
Vobster Inn 99
Waggon & Horses **27**, 27, 37, 38
Wells Way Inn **28**

quarrying 16, 56, 63, **126-9**

Radstock 125
Richmont Castle 86
Rickford 35, 150
riding **164**
rivers
  Axe 52, 101, 123, 133
  Sheppey 78, 80, 83
  Yeo 62
roads
  A361 19, 29, 38
  A368 19, 28, 35
  A37 19, 20
  A371 26
  A38 19, 29
  B3135 19, 26
  B3139 27
  Old Bristol Road 28
  Old Wells Road 32
'Rock of Ages' 71
Rodney Stoke 13, 19, **95-6**, 109, 143
Romans 46
Rowberrow 11, 34, 48, **96**, 124, 164
Rowberrow Camp 96
Rowberrow Warren 34
Royal Forest of Mendip 10, 60, 61

Saxons 46-7
Scott of the Antarctic 88
Scott, Sir Gilbert 56, 73, 98
Sedgemoor 53
Sedgemoor, Battle of 51, 65, 123
set-aside 104
Sharcome Grange 80
sheep 12
sheep see Golden Fleece 48
Sheldon, David **141-7**, *142*

Shepherd, David 40, 58, 78
Shepton Mallet 11, 19, 21, 22, 38, 40, 46, 50, 52, 57, 58, **63-6**
Shepton Mallet Caving Club 148
Shipham 16, 23, 34, 43, 52, 53, 71, **97**, 124, 143, 162, 164
Shipham Equestrian Centre 164
Showerings 22, 64
Shute Shelve Hill 19
Site of Special Scientific Interest 104, **104-5**, 108, 110, 114, 131
Small, Bill **135-41**, *136*
Smitham Chimney 87, *116*
Smitham Hill 16
Smitham Hill Mineries 119
Soho 38, 39
Somerset & Dorset Canal 56
Somerset & Dorset Railway 57, 70
Somerset County Council 127
Somerset Trust for Nature Conservation 32
Somerset Trust Reserve 24
Somerset Wildlife Trust 108, **109**, 110, 126, 136, 155, 158
Somersetshire Regiment 51
Somerville, Sir James 80
SSSI *see* Site of Special Scientific Interest
St. Aldhelm 47, 81
St. Aldhelm's Well 63, 82
St. Cuthbert's Church, Wells 69
St. Cuthbert's Mine 55
St. Cuthbert's Lead Works 123, 124
St. Cuthbert's Paper Mill 50
Steep Holm 10, 11, 23, 24
Stoke Bottom 98
Stoke Bottom Hill 52
Stoke Lane 56
Stoke St. Michael **97-8**, 134
Ston Easton 84, 121
Stratton-on-the-Fosse 38, 39, 54, 56, 76, **98-9**, 125
strawberries 13-4, 53, 63, 82, **141-7**
strawberry country **29-31**
Strawberry Fair 82
Strawberry Line 82
Strode, Edward 51
sump 132
swallet holes 11, 16, 129

Toplady, Rev. Augustus 71
Torr Quarry 127
Treaty of Wedmore 47
Tudway Estate 111

WEST COUNTRY LANDSCAPES
series:

THE SOMERSET LEVELS
by Robin & Romey Williams
'Comprehensive, rounded and up to date – the author's knowledge of the area shines through.'
176 pages; Photographs and pen & ink drawings; Price £6.95

THE VALE OF PEWSEY
by John Chandler
'With deep affection and a wealth of knowledge, John Chandler gives us the heart of Wiltshire. We could not have a better guide, the first book to describe the Vale of Pewsey for nearly 40 years ... this excellent book.'
160 pages; Numerous photographs and maps; Price £6.95

THE MARLBOROUGH DOWNS
by Kenneth Watts
This book is surely the one which the region has long deserved. It provides a fascinating companion for anyone who, to quote Richard Jefferies, has been drawn by 'the blue hill lines, the dark copses on the ridges, the shadows in the combes' which typify the Marlborough Downs.
192 pages; Fully illustrated; Price £7.95

THE LIMPLEY STOKE VALLEY
by Margaret Wilson
The first book to be devoted to this unique corner of the West Country for many years; it will surely establish itself as a thorough and enjoyable source of reference for many years to come.
160 pages; Fully illustrated; Price £7.95

MENDIP RAMBLES
by Peter Wright
The 12 circular rambles described in this book, of around five miles each, guide you about a region of hill country which is a lesser known face of the green and pleasant land of Somerset.
Peter Wright's keen sense of history, curiosity about all he observes and sympathy with the natural world engages the reader and rambler throughout. The perfect companion for exploring Mendip on foot.
'The multi-faceted character of Mendip is caught splendidly ... this very informative and practical handbook.'
80 pages; maps and drawings; Price £3.95

COUNTRY BOOKSHELF *is a list of around a dozen titles which cover various aspects of rural life; they are all illustrated paperbacks, attractively presented, and all cost less than £5.*

EX LIBRIS PRESS *books are available through your local bookshop or direct from the publisher, post-free, on receipt of net price, at:*

*1 The Shambles
Bradford on Avon
Wiltshire   BA15 1JS
Tel\ Fax 01225 863595*

Please ask for a copy of our free, illustrated catalogue which feature around 50 titles on the West Country, rural life and the Channel Islands.